❖ ❖ ❖

An Invitation to "Go Deeper"

Much more than a "how-to manual," the UNBOUND MINISTRY Guidebook invites each reader to go deeper into the Heart of the Father.

I encourage everyone reading this book to be open to the "new things" the Holy Spirit will reveal to you as you more fully embrace the loving call of Jesus to serve Him in setting the captives free—including yourself!

— Nancy Greenhaw
G.R.A.C.E. Ministries

UNBOUND MINISTRY Guidebook

Helping Others Find Freedom in Christ

NEAL LOZANO

& Matthew Lozano

Jubilee Studio

CLINTON CORNERS, NEW YORK

UNBOUND MINISTRY Guidebook: Helping Others Find Freedom in Christ

Copyright © 2011 by Neal Lozano and Matthew Lozano

All rights reserved. No part of this publication may be reproduced, stored in a retrieval system, or transmitted in any form or by any means—electronic, mechanical, photocopy, recording, or any other—except for brief quotations in printed reviews, without the prior permission of the publisher.

Published by:
JUBILEE STUDIO, P.O. Box 75, Clinton Corners, NY 12514. Jubilee Studio is an imprint of The Attic Studio Publishing House. Phone: 845-266-8100; E-mail: atticstudiopress@aol.com

in collaboration with:
HEART OF THE FATHER MINISTRIES, P.O. Box 905, Ardmore, PA 19003. Phone: 610-952-3019; website: www.heartofthefather.com

Book and cover design by Ted Schluenderfritz ▪ www.5Sparrows.com

Cover photo by Savas Keskiner

Unless otherwise noted, all Scripture references are taken from the Revised Standard Version of the Bible, copyright 1952 [2nd edition, 1971] by the Division of Christian Education of the National Council of the Churches of Christ in the United States of America. Used by permission. All rights reserved.

Scripture marked NIV is taken from the HOLY BIBLE, NEW INTERNATIONAL VERSION®. NIV®. Copyright © 1973, 1978, 1984 by International Bible Society. Used by permission of Zondervan. All rights reserved.

Scripture quotations marked NLT are taken from the Holy Bible, New Living Translation, copyright © 1996, 2004, 2007. Used by permission of Tyndale House Publishers Inc., Carol Stream, Illinois 60188. All rights reserved.

Disclaimer: Although the authors and publisher have made every effort to ensure the accuracy and completeness of the information shared in this book, neither shall be liable for errors, omissions, inaccuracies or inconsistencies. Nor is it their intent to act as medical or professional counsel.

ISBN: 978-1-883551-25-4

Printed in the United States of America

Table of Contents

A Letter from Neal Lozano VII
Introduction: Sharing Your Encounter with Jesus. XI

Part I
SONS AND DAUGHTERS OF GOD 1
CHAPTER 1. *God Delights in You*. 3
CHAPTER 2. *The Necessity of the Holy Spirit* 15
CHAPTER 3. *Humility: The Nature of Christ* 25
CHAPTER 4. *Compassion: The Heart of Christ* 35

Part II
RELEASING THE GIFT OF FREEDOM 47
CHAPTER 5. *Listening* 49
CHAPTER 6. *Recognizing the Enemy*. 59
CHAPTER 7. *Understanding Foundational Patterns* 71
CHAPTER 8. *Self-Justification* 85
CHAPTER 9. *Speaking the Father's Blessing* 95

Part III
MAKING SENSE OF UNBOUND (FAQS) 105
CHAPTER 10. *Growing in Leadership*. 109
CHAPTER 11. *Ministry Issues*. 119
CHAPTER 12. *Why Unbound Differs From Other Deliverance Models* 145

Appendix Contents 165

Appendix A
UNBOUND READINGS. 167
Testimonies 167
Sample Ministry Session 179

Appendix B
UNBOUND MINISTRY TOOLS. 199

Postscript
The Way Forward. 229

A Letter from Neal Lozano

Dear Friends in Christ,

Thank you for continuing with us in this exciting adventure as, together, we seek to faithfully serve the One who sets the captives free.

For more than 40 years, I have experienced the great privilege and joy of helping others find freedom in Christ. The Gospel truly is good news! Traveling with teams both near and far, my wife Janet and I have so often witnessed the profound power of God's love and truth in utilizing the Five Keys of UNBOUND. As has been said by more than one participant, "The ministry of UNBOUND is a place 'where the rubber meets the road' in our journey with the Lord."

WHERE DO WE GO FROM HERE?
The Boundless Possibilities

Over the past decade, the message of the Five Keys of UNBOUND has been carried around the world in ways we could never have imagined. Some have told me that when they travel, they bring copies of *UNBOUND: A Practical Guide to Deliverance* in order to spread the good news of UNBOUND to different nations. With the publication of *Resisting the Devil: A Catholic Perspective on Deliverance* in 2010, new doors are opening for us to bring the message to Catholic seminarians, clergy, and bishops. **We planted the first seed; many of you have**

planted more; the planting will continue. This Ministry Guidebook is intended to cultivate and nourish the young seedlings so they will produce good fruit in the Kingdom of God.

UNBOUND MINISTRY releases the power of the gospel in a form that is easily understood and reproduced. Many groups have adopted the ministry and are now promoting the book more effectively than any marketing professional could. People hear about the freedom others have received. When they ask for help, they are often invited to read *UNBOUND* as preparation for a ministry session.

SHARING THE MESSAGE OF THE FIVE KEYS:
A Variety of Approaches

As the message of the Five Keys continues to spread, we are able to identify two basic ministry categories emerging. On the one hand, there are those who use the UNBOUND model as "a tool in their spiritual tool chest," integrating it with other approaches to ministry. We are happy to be able to contribute in this way. On the other hand, there are those who are more singularly focused on using the UNBOUND model, receiving training to be part of formalized UNBOUND MINISTRY teams.

Both groups are legitimate. The main issue is that each group needs to identify its approach so that people coming for ministry know exactly what form of ministry they are going to receive. In this way, the integrity of UNBOUND MINISTRY can be preserved, while allowing a wide use of the principles by people beyond those who are officially aligned with the UNBOUND model.

To that end, we ask that if you use the UNBOUND model in combination with other approaches to healing and deliverance, you call your ministry something different so as to distinguish it from UNBOUND MINISTRY. If you have a healing, renewal, or transformation center and UNBOUND is *one* of the many ministries that you offer, please make the distinctions clear so seekers can choose what type of ministry they desire. In some instances, there may also be those who miss a piece of what we teach and thereby misrepresent the principles and the values of UNBOUND MINISTRY. If we are to increase as a movement that reaches people around the world and influences many parts of the church, we need consistency in what others present as UNBOUND MINISTRY (or the Five Keys).[1]

As is the case with this *UNBOUND MINISTRY Guidebook* (emerging from our shared experiences over the years), every aspect of the UNBOUND model has been carefully reviewed and tested. There is a reason behind each of the core points of what we teach and why all the keys are integrated into one approach to inner healing and deliverance. We have resisted complicating the UNBOUND model with elements and teachings that are not part of the basic core. We've seen that those who have been most successful in using and spreading the message have stuck to the simplicity of what we have taught. One leader noted, "I learned the most by sticking to the model, using all five keys. I grew in my understanding of them as I used them." Another person, after watching Janet and me minister to someone, said, "The difference between you and all the other people I have observed using the Five Keys is that you and Janet trust in the keys and do not go beyond them."

The *UNBOUND MINISTRY Guidebook* builds upon what was written in the second part of *UNBOUND* and I trust it will be an encouragement to all those using the Five Keys to help others. **I believe that what is in this book is vital to keeping us on course and empowering people to set the captives free in a way that continues to be reproducible in different parts of the church and among the nations.**

Among the many dedicated co-laborers over the years who have contributed their wisdom, insights and experiences to the *MINISTRY Guidebook*, I would especially like to thank my son, Matthew,

---

[1] You will find a clear discussion of what constitutes UNBOUND MINISTRY on our website, www.heartofthefather.com. We urge you to visit us online as you plan your own ministry. Our website offers a wealth of material to serve those involved in Unbound Ministry, including a document, "Using the Unbound Name."

who collaborated with me in preparing this book and wrote two of its chapters. He is currently assisting UNBOUND leaders as they develop local ministries.

> *Blessed be the God and Father of our Lord Jesus Christ, the Father of mercies and God of all comfort, who comforts us in all our affliction, so that we may be able to comfort those who are in any affliction, with the comfort with which we ourselves are comforted by God.*
>
> 2 Corinthians 1:3-4

May the Lord use the time you spend with this guidebook to bring you into a deeper encounter with the truth of His love for you, so that you may become a more perfect vessel of His liberating power to those who are in need.

In the Father's Love,

Neal Lozano

This book is dedicated to our faithful friend, Joseph Marchese, who served with us from the beginning of Heart of the Father Ministries. He went home to be with the Lord on July 6, 2011, as this Guidebook was being written. His faith, love, joy, and humble service are a lasting legacy which he has imparted to all of us who served with him.

Introduction
Sharing Your Encounter with Jesus

You were delivered. You found freedom. Perhaps your breakthrough came at an UNBOUND: Freedom in Christ conference. Perhaps it came as you read *UNBOUND: A Practical Guide to Deliverance.* It may have happened last year or five years ago, but however or whenever you received deliverance, now you want to give it away. This is the door to greater freedom.

Everyone who has received from God can give. In fact, God expects us to give freely what we have received (see Matthew 10:8). One man who experienced liberation during the pre-conference training returned to his office thirty minutes later and used the Five Keys as he prayed with a furloughing missionary. The missionary was set free as well. Another, a man who had been a psychotherapist for twenty-five years, became a regular member of our ministry team after receiving his freedom. He testified that though he had helped many people over those years, now that he prayed with them using the UNBOUND model, he saw them healed and set free. This, he said, was a greater privilege.

Never forget the privilege you have of releasing the power of the gospel into the darkness of a man or a woman's heart. Remember the encounters you have had with God and what He has done as you have led others to the freedom Jesus brings. Remembering will motivate you to greater dedication, releasing deeper understanding, and provoking a readiness to make sacrifices to serve those who come to you for help. Janet and I remember so many of God's children who have received freedom through UNBOUND and through Heart of the Father Ministries. We remember the broken man, unable to look Janet in the eye because of terrible childhood abuse and years of living under the shame. We remember his inability to be touched; we remember the complete change when he allowed Janet to hug him after the Father's blessing. We remember the tormented woman whose great-grandmother had been a psychic; we remember her happiness as she spoke of her experience of the Father's love. And we remember Clair, a committed Christian and successful professional whose life was ruined by the lie that she would make a mistake that would ruin everything and cause those who loved her to abandon her. We will always remember how Clair stood up with confidence at her church and testified publicly to her freedom.

Now, what will they remember? Will the man remember the respect Janet gave in gently asking to touch his hand? Will the tormented woman remember the lack of fear about the occult and how gently Jesus came to set her free? Will Clair remember the understanding, the acceptance, and the lack of judgment? Will she remember the way I stumbled over some of the words I used to lead her—which will remind her that God will cover over her mistakes if her heart is right? In each interaction, we sought not to follow a method or perform a job well; we sought to follow Jesus' heart in loving each person as we were guided by the Five Keys. It is likely that they will remember the little things we do with love and they will remember the big thing God does—which will be their motivation to seek deeper freedom for themselves and those they love.

Ministry Deepens

The word *ministry* means "service." Whether you occasionally have an opportunity to help a friend or are part of a team that provides UNBOUND ministry, the quality of your service needs to continue to deepen. As you learn to lead UNBOUND teams and pray with more and more people, you will need much more than information; you will need active faith, sincere compassion, deep humility, and utter dependence on the leading of the Holy Spirit. The purpose of this guidebook is to equip you and further propel you into a model of ministry that took us many years to learn. This is a resource that you may read and reread through the years as you serve those who come to you. Our prayer is that this guidebook will take you deeper into the treasures the Father has for you as you learn to love others well. We invite you into the process of going deeper with the Lord.

The journey begins here: with your understanding that deliverance and freedom are never one-time experiences. Just as the Scriptures talk about salvation as a past event, a daily present deliverance, and our future hope, so freedom is much greater than an experience. It is the ongoing flooding of the soul with the awareness of God's love and mercy. It is also the promise of the glory that we will know someday—the glory of being always in the presence of God and experiencing the fullness of His love. This is why Paul prays for the Ephesians—and for us—that they may know this love.

> *For this reason I kneel before the Father, from whom His whole family in heaven and on earth derives its name. I pray that out of His glorious riches He may strengthen you with power through His Spirit in your inner being, so that Christ may dwell in your hearts through faith. And I pray that you, being rooted and established in love, may have power, together with all the saints, to grasp how wide and long and high and deep is the love that surpasses knowledge—that you may be filled to the measure of all the fullness of God.*
>
> Ephesians 3:14-19 (NIV)

That is our prayer for you as well. As men and women who minister under the Lordship of Jesus Christ, each of us is in need of His daily deliverance, in need of the Lord's presence. For this reason, we begin this guidebook by addressing the foundational issues for sons and daughters of God: faith, hope, and love in the Holy Spirit. You will find them in my book, UNBOUND, like threads of different colors woven through a tapestry. Here they are addressed directly. If you have been seeking the Lord through the years, I am confident that God has been weaving His fruit into your life, for He is faithful. He has been preparing you for ministry long before you could see what He was preparing you for, just as the foundation is poured and set long before neighborhood watchers have any idea what a house will look like.

The most important foundation for ministry is your own full participation in the heart of the Father—in His delight in you (Chapter 1).

This truth empowers you to speak the Father's blessing into the hearts of those to whom you minister and imparts to you a greater ability to give away what the Lord gives you. For this truth to work deep into your heart and spill over into the lives of others, it is essential you learn to trust the Holy Spirit in all things and listen to His voice (Chapter 2). Above all, seek after compassion and humility (Chapters 3 and 4), for this love is His will:

> *Put on then, as God's chosen ones, holy and beloved, compassion, kindness, lowliness, meekness, and patience, forbearing one another and, if one has a complaint against another, forgiving each other; as the Lord has forgiven you, so you also must forgive. And above all these put on love, which binds everything together in perfect harmony.*
> Colossians 3:12-14

As you read these first four chapters, I pray you are led to a deeper hunger to be like Christ in your ministry and to be more fully a vessel of God's love.

Ministry Helps

Part II of this guidebook offers practical teaching on implementing the UNBOUND model. As you listen to God and the one He sends to you, you will find the Five Keys increasingly effective (Chapter 5), you will gain greater insight into the enemies' strategies, which will lead you to have greater success in assisting a person in need to name their enemies (Chapter 6), and you will gain a deeper understanding of the human heart (Chapter 7).

Chapter 8 focuses on exposing the work of self-justification, a basic response of man's fallen nature, while Chapter 9 gives suggestions and examples to help you effectively speak the Father's blessing into the lives of those who have been set free.

Part III serves as an FAQ reference guide as you use and teach the UNBOUND model, but it is much more than simply answers to questions. By adding my "further reflections" to each question, I give you the opportunity for deeper understanding of the answer and related issues.

Finally, the Appendices contain additional material that will expand your understanding of the UNBOUND model and extend your ability to help others find freedom. Appendix A contains four testimonies that add depth to topics addressed in Chapter 4 and Questions 8, 9, and 14. You will also find a ministry session that was transcribed so you can see how the Five Keys were applied. Appendix B contains practical materials on discernment of spirits, lists of lies and spirits, and other documents that you can reproduce or download from our website. We conclude with a Postscript that points the way forward.

Ask the Lord for Guidance

We thank the Lord for using you to draw people to the Father, where they will find the truth that every human being longs for: the truth that God calls them sons and daughters, the truth that He delights in them. As you begin to minister, ask the Lord to be your guide. You may be tempted to read for information and to categorize what you read as valuable or not. I invite you to read asking the Holy Spirit to teach you. Some things I say will be too much for you to implement now. Just leave them with the Lord as you whisper, "Lord, please teach me about that." He will in time. When you reread a page or a chapter, you will be surprised at the ways He has answered your simple prayer of faith.

The Lord will continue to build you into a house of welcome and a doorway to freedom for others. One of my favorite passages is from Psalm 26: "Lord, I love the house where you live, the place where your glory dwells." (verse 8 NIV).

As you delight daily in His presence, as you seek to dwell in His heart, remember that being a house, a place of ministry, is first being a place for Him to dwell: "If a man loves Me, he will keep My Word, and My Father will love him, and We will come to him and make Our home with him" (John 14:23).

PART I
SONS AND DAUGHTERS OF GOD

Blessed are the peacemakers, they shall be called sons of the living God. (MATTHEW 5:9, paraphrased)

As sons and daughters of God we are called to do His work, reconciling man to God and reconciling persons in the human family. God's work is not something we simply do; it flows from who we are. To do His work we must be God-like. In Biblical times a son represented his father not only in his business but also in his person. The words of Jesus would have made perfect sense in His culture: "He who has seen me has seen the Father" (John 14:9).

If you are doing the work of a peacemaker using the UNBOUND model, be confident that as God works through you He is going deeper in you, producing in you the qualities of a son or daughter of God. Each of the first four chapters will give you the opportunity to ask yourself one of the following key questions and to dive deeply into the answer. Do you know that God delights in you? Do you rely on the Holy Spirit? Is humility your path? Is it compassion that moves you? Before we learn more in Part 2 about releasing the gift of freedom in others, we will consider our own freedom as children of God, who, knowing the Heart of the Father, are thereby equipped to serve as Jesus served. God is working in us as He works through us. God is able to do both simultaneously with ultimate efficiency. We who wish to do what the Father is doing must be careful to keep in balance these two areas, God's work in others and God's work in us, not neglecting the one for the other.

Chapter 1
God Delights in You
BY MATTHEW LOZANO

The Lord your God is with you, He is mighty to save.
He will take great delight in you, He will quiet you with His love,
He will rejoice over you with singing. (ZEPHANIAH 3:17 NIV)

Here is some good news: God likes you! He really, really likes you! This is the fundamental reality of who you are in Christ and the essence of your life as a son or daughter of God. Do you want to minister like Jesus, setting the captives free? Then you need to understand that Jesus' authority to heal and deliver came from His perfect relationship with the Father. The power to heal and deliver can only come from the same place—from your union with the Father through Jesus, His Son. The Father imparted to Jesus *His* fundamental reality by expressing the pleasure of His heart: "This is My beloved Son, with whom I am well pleased. Listen to Him!" Notice, the Father didn't say, "Listen to Jesus—He's really holy!" Instead, the starting point of Jesus' public ministry began with the Father's declaration that His Son was a great pleasure to Him. This declaration became a wellspring of strength and authority, as pleasing the Father was the motivation for all of Jesus' great works.

It gets better: As we embrace our identity as ransomed and adopted children of God, we too lay claim to the blessing and inheritance that belongs to Jesus. Take in the Father's words as I paraphrase His blessing over you: "This is My beloved child, in whom I delight. This is the love of My heart; My favor rests on you. Son, you please Me well. Daughter, you fill Me with joy."

The Father's delight in us is not just a happy thought. It is the Creator's *original disposition* toward us as His greatest creation. The purpose of Jesus' life, death, and resurrection was to restore a right relationship between a loving Father and His wayward children by destroying the power of sin, enabling us to trust Him and experience His delight. Furthermore, knowing His delight is a *key to life* and it enables us to walk in obedience, handle tough circumstances, and fulfill our call and destiny. Our ability as a redeemed creature to experience God's pleasure and love becomes a wellspring of motivation to minister to others, to set the captives free.

The problem is many of us do not want to accept the thought that we please God. For some, the idea of God's love as a virtue or theological principle is okay, but the idea that God actually *likes* us is hard to handle. We identify with the sin in our lives and see ourselves as shameful sinners who are merely accepted because of Jesus. God therefore tolerates us, holding His nose like an uncomfortable dad with a stinky, diapered infant. One problem with this thinking is that we identify with the very sin Jesus came to remove and reject the identity He came to bestow. We are not called to participate in the old self but to put on Christ and live in the power of His resurrection—we are a new creation. By adopting us as children, God invites us to participate in His life and in His nature.

Delight Is the Nature of God

To *delight* means "to take great pleasure; to experience great satisfaction or gratification." Because of His perfection, God is, by nature, completely delighted in Himself. He dwells in an unbroken, eternal family relationship, in complete and utter pleasure. There is no pleasure like that experienced between the Father, the Son, and the Spirit. Proverbs gives us a prophetic picture of this eternal delight: "Then I was the craftsman at His side. I was filled with delight day after day, rejoicing always in His presence, rejoicing in His whole world and delighting in mankind" (Proverbs 8:30-31 NIV).

God expressed His complete joy through creation. Ponder this: God created all people—including you—from His delight and *for* His delight. You were made to be His companion, a person like Him but not Him. This is the great generosity and vulnerability of God, who wants another to experience Him and know Him intimately. Being made in His image enables you to experience communion with Him, to feel what He feels. Furthermore, you are also given the ability to freely and deeply love Him in return. Each man, each woman, is a person capable of thrilling God's heart with endless delight.

How do we know God is thrilled? Because He stopped creating. God did not look at us and say, "Let Me try that again." Rather, God made man at the very end of the creative process and when He looked at the whole of His creation He then said, "It is *very* good!" God is very creative (I'm a big fan of His work), and He certainly would have made us differently if He needed to. But He didn't. He was delighted with us as the final touch of His creation. So He chose to stop working and begin enjoying. He walked in His creation and had fellowship with Adam and Eve in the cool of the day.

Have you ever wondered why God placed man in a garden? First, because a garden is a place of intentional order, where caring nurture provides the opportunity for life to grow and flourish. But second, a garden is intended for the pleasure of the gardener. Having finished all his work, the gardener wants to enjoy what his imagination has created. This is particularly true of Adam and Eve who were the pinnacle of that creative process. They were made in the Gardener's image and He wanted to enjoy communion with them. This is the reason God chose to dwell in it.

If you are designed to know and respond to His delight in you, then what happens when you reject the truth that He delights in you? The answer is you don't know Him fully. You can know of His power and His majesty, His beauty and His wisdom, but if you don't know what delights Him so profoundly, you have missed the essence of who God is and the source of His motivation. You have missed the heart of the Father. I've been to several funerals where someone has said something like, "You really don't know Bob unless you know he loved fly fishing." I often walked away from these funerals feeling like I knew the person better because a friend had revealed the source of his passion. It is the same with God. When you miss the source of His passion, you miss His heart. When you miss His heart, you misunderstand the Person.

You Are His Bride

The apostle Paul echoed the heart of God for His people when he prayed for the Ephesians "that you may be filled to the measure of all the fullness of God" (Ephesians 3:19b NIV). What is another word for *fullness*? *Delight!* Delight is extreme gratification and satisfaction. Paul's prayer is that we find fullness in God's fullness and pleasure from His pleasure over us. Read his prayer again as I paraphrase: "that you may be gratified to the measure of the gratification of God, delighted to the measure of the delight of God, and satisfied to the measure of His satisfaction." You see? He wants you to experience His delight. He wants you to feel, experience, and live in His satisfied heart. This transformational reality enables you to love Him in return.

St. John writes, "We love because He first loved us" (1 John 4:19 NIV). His love initiates your love. His love unlocks your heart. When you receive His delight as the truth about who you are, you are empowered to love. In Ephesians 5, Paul writes about a key image which describes the relationship between Christ and His church: that of a bridegroom and his bride. The word *delight* comes from the Latin word meaning "to allure" or "to entice." A bride is enchanting to her bridegroom and he is drawn to her. As the bride of Christ, you intoxicate God and He is drawn to you.

A bride is one who receives the knowledge of the bridegroom's delight and embraces it as her identity. She responds in freedom and boldness because she knows she is pleasing and is secure in the love of the beloved. She neither responds out of the fear of disappointing him nor tries to offer obedience in exchange for favors. The bridegroom showers his love on his bride, and she responds out of the deep understanding that she is satisfying. She does not have to guess what pleases him; she only needs to give the gift of herself. Loving God is not simply about righteous behavior. Loving God means knowing and experiencing His pleasure and living in the knowledge of what pleases

Him. As you move with His heart and grow closer to His heart, you mature as a lover of God.

Sin, Shame, and Unworthiness

Sin, of course, separated mankind from this reality, spoiling freedom and distorting our perception of God. Sin took Adam and Eve from the garden of delight to a place of hard toil and obstacles. Their first response was one of shame; they covered themselves out of fear. You too, when you were lost in sin, related to God with suspicion and the fear of punishment. Because you identified with sin, God could not enjoy the delight of His heart. The Old Testament prophets show us the pain of a bridegroom who longs for his bride to become responsive to his love. An unresponsive bride offers sacrifice and token obedience when the bridegroom only wants her!

Even in the state of your worst sin, however, you never stopped being the source of God's delight. He continues to delight in the person you were created to be. In fact, the very wrath of God is directed toward sin because it separates Him from the object of His love. The intensity of God's anger is actually a measure of His passion for you. This great desire and furious anger met at the cross—where Jesus dealt forever with the barrier of sin.

Now that you have been redeemed from sin and reconciled to God through faith in Jesus, why do you still struggle with the idea He actually enjoys you? Why is it hard for you to respond freely and boldly from the heart? The answer, for many, is a faulty sense of unworthiness. Now don't get me wrong—no one ever deserved God's mercy. No measure of justice would have declared us innocent. In this sense, we are right to say we were not worthy, or *deserving*, of the gift we have received. However, we often fail to honor another definition of worth. *Worth* is also defined by the value—or price—that is paid for something. Hebrews 12 tells us Jesus, "for the joy set before Him, endured the cross." God the Son measured out the price of His precious blood in exchange for an eternity with you. Do you know what this means? He chose *you*. What was the "joy" (delight) set before Him? His bride. You are worthy by the measure of His love. If He loves you this much, then you must be lovely.

Many of us confuse what we deserve with our value. We choose to measure ourselves by what we have done rather than what He has done for us. But Jesus was not a fool to die for you. Who are you to claim that you have no value when He has declared your great worth on the cross? Can you deny the glorious Son of God the deepest desire of His heart? Why settle for your own self-judgment when He has called you His joy?

SIGNS OF THE STRUGGLE

Unless you accept the reality of God's delight in you, it will be difficult for you to mature in love. In the Old Testament, there is the tragic figure of King Saul, chosen by God to be the first king of Israel and yet he never fully trusted in God. We can identity five symptoms that reveal Saul's inability to accept God's love and delight in him. As you read about each symptom in his story, ask the Holy Spirit to reveal if you, like Saul, need to know His delight.

1. *Unworthiness and shame:* Do you refuse to receive the revelation that you are lovely and desirable? When Samuel found Saul to anoint him king over Israel, Saul's response was: "But am I not a Benjamite, from the smallest tribe of Israel, and is not my clan the least of all the clans of the tribe of Benjamin? Why do you say such a thing to me?" (1 Samuel 9:21 NIV). Saul did not have the spiritual formation that he needed to be king—a kingship that was forced upon him by an anxious people who did not want God's will. He saw himself as unworthy, and he acted from a sense of unworthiness and shame throughout his life.

2. *Fearing the displeasure of others more than God's displeasure:* When God's pleasure has not touched your heart, it is easier for other things to come in and motivate you. Are you motivated to please other people more than God? Saul sure was. God gave him a simple task—destroy the enemy and take no spoils (1 Samuel 15:3). But Saul could not say 'no' to the people. He allowed the people to keep spoils because he feared their displeasure more than God's (1 Samuel 15:24). God's pleasure had not permeated his heart to the point where he was able to say, "Nothing is more important than

Your desires; nothing is more important than pleasing You." When Samuel came and tried to correct him, Saul lied, self-justified, and then finally begged for forgiveness only when the fear of punishment took over.

3. *Misinterpreting God's intentions for your circumstances.* God's intention was for Saul to repent. He took away His Spirit and sent an evil spirit to torment him, to cause him to see the destruction in his life and to agree with what the Lord had said through Samuel—that he would no longer be king (1 Samuel 16:14). But Saul misinterpreted God's heart in the matter. He interpreted it as a rejection of himself—not as discipline. Saul felt the loving hand of God (who grieved for Saul) as if it were punishment. Instead of looking forward to his future calling, Saul felt abandoned. Because Saul was not close to God's heart, he could not see that the correction, discipline, and rebuke were working in love for him, so he did everything he could to hang onto his kingdom in opposition to God's direct Word.

4. *Missing God's heart and His secrets.* God has secrets for you—things He wants to say in the secret place that only you can hear. He wants to share what is in His heart. He won't share his secrets with anybody else and He won't share them with someone who is not after His heart. (David, unlike Saul, was just that sort of man). As with the first human, God wanted to meet Saul in his inner garden and delight in Saul, but Saul could not hear. He saw God's delight in David as an affront to him: charming, spiritual, fearless David would take his kingdom. God's purpose was not to humiliate Saul. Rather, His purpose was to turn his heart, to get Saul to say, "Me too, Lord. I want a close relationship with You. I want to know Your delight." When God brings hard circumstances to you, this is His purpose. He wants you to be jealous for His heart.

5. *Putting your position over your identity.* After all, the best substitute for unmerited love and joy is a "good old position" over other people, right? No man ever tried to wrest Saul's position from him. David refused to touch the Lord's anointed and even Samuel, with all his power, left the crown in Saul's hands. But Saul still fought to

protect his crown and his reputation even as David continued to rise (1 Samuel 18:8). Your heart was not designed to be satisfied with power or titles. Your heart was made to experience God's love. Jesus told His disciples to be like little children sitting in their father's embrace. Young children do not worry about titles or a pecking order. They revel in the knowledge that Mom and Dad love them.

The Ravished Heart

In contrast to Saul, we have the story of David. Here was a man who was both a mighty warrior and a heartsick lover and friend of God. His mission was to fight his enemies, expand his kingdom, and create the environment for the dwelling place of God. He swooned in God's presence and yearned for God's presence like a thirsty deer. God called David "a man after My own heart" because David's heart was ravished by God. God's pleasure over his life was his greatest treasure. He understood that no matter what his circumstance or his failures were, God was for him. What was true of David can be true for you too.

Over time, God's grace begins to work deeply in our hearts. As you let your heart be ravished by God's love, you will begin to experience the following in your life.

1. *Shame no longer dominates you, and the fear of punishment goes away.* Have you noticed how the people in the Bible who loved God did not keep very good records of their sins? David was intensely aware of his sin. He was a murderer and an adulterer, but when he confessed his sin, he knew it was gone. How else could David write, "God has rewarded me according to the cleanness of my hands"? Did he suffer from memory loss? No, he understood the Father's love. Perfect love *drives out fear* because fear has to do with punishment (1 John 4:18 NIV). When we are motivated by the love of God rather than the fear of punishment, we can humbly repent when we fail. We can earnestly seek God, knowing that he is pleased by faith and rewards it (Hebrews 11:6).

2. *You become bold in the face of adversity.* When Goliath mocked young David and came at him with the sword, David faced the giant without fear because he knew without a doubt that God loved

him. He knew God "rescued him because He delighted in him" (Psalm 18:19, paraphrased). The entire life of David was a series of God's rescue missions—from bears, lions, kings, and even the hand of David's own son. David knew nothing could stop God from pursuing the delight of His heart.

3. *The opinions of others do not determine your actions.* David danced before the Lord—right out of his clothes (2 Samuel 6:14-22). His wife called him a shame and a disgrace, and was embarrassed by his lack of propriety. But you know what? David didn't care. "You haven't seen anything yet," he said. David knew he was delighting God. If you weigh the pleasure of God on one end of a scale and the fear of judgment or embarrassment on the other, the weight of His pleasure always wins. Consider this: would you take your spouse to the finest sushi bar in the world with the highest ratings and reviews, knowing your spouse hates sushi? Do you want the approval of others or the pleasure of the one you love? The more we experience His delight, the less we will be distracted by the judgments of others. We become motivated by what pleases Him.

4. *You become jealous over the secret place you have with God.* When you experience God's delight, you are jealous over your relationship with Him and do not give it up for lesser distractions. Sin loses its attractiveness because it steals you away from Him.

5. *You learn to know God's heart.* As you lean on His heart, God will reveal more of Himself to you. You will notice that the greatest revelations in Scripture were revealed to those who knew God's delight and sought deep friendship with Him. Moses was a man who would not move without the presence of the Lord. David longed for the Lord like a thirsty deer. John leaned upon the Lord's breast and sought the deep things of Jesus' heart. Because of this intimacy with the Lord, each man was given a special revelation. Moses received prophetic insight about the identity and the future of the tribes of Israel. David was given prophetic instruction about the construction of the temple, as well as psalms that would foreshadow the coming Messiah. John was granted revelation about

God's heavenly kingdom and coming judgments. God wants to give you more and share the secrets of His heart with you.

6. *You are enabled to take risks in the pursuit of His glory.* David spent his entire life seeking God's glory. His heart's desire was to build a place for God to dwell, and he spent his fortune, his armies, and his sweat to prepare for it. When you know God takes pleasure in you, your ability to take risks for His kingdom is released. You can step out in faith to love others, seek your calling, and fulfill your destiny.

7. *Your pleasure becomes tied to His.* You delight in pleasing Him. David knew the heart of God. He knew God wanted nothing more than to dwell with His people, so David wanted nothing more than to build God a temple. But God said no. David was rejected because he was a man of war (1 Chronicles 28:3). So now his whole mission in life, his very destiny, seemed to be for naught. How did David respond? Rather than interpreting this as Saul did, David turned his vision and his inheritance over to his son, Solomon. He gathered everything that was needed to build the temple and got it all ready for Solomon. When David died, Solomon built the temple. David prepared this work for a generation he would never see. The purpose for his life had become part of the eternal plan of God for His people.

David fulfilled his destiny through Solomon because he lived in the reality of God's delight. It became his pleasure to seek God's pleasure beyond his position and circumstances, knowing that "goodness and mercy will follow me all the days of my life, and I will dwell in the house of the Lord forever" (Psalm 23:6, paraphrased). Let this be the reality of your life. As you seek to minister to others, let the pleasure of God over your life bring you to a place of boldness and authority, motivating and encouraging you to call forth the responsive bride in others. Most importantly, I pray you will enjoy Him as He enjoys you every day of your life.

Let me exhort you to give the Lord what He wants. Jesus Christ wants you more than anything else you could offer. He wants you more than your service, your acts of obedience, and your ministry to others.

Start giving Him permission to delight in you. In your quiet place, say to Him, "Lord, take delight in me; enjoy me." Offer yourself for His goodwill and pleasure. Then be jealous for what belongs to Him. Guard the knowledge of His delight and don't let judgments or circumstances tell you otherwise. In humility, embrace the truth that God delights in you and you will have what you need to speak the Father's blessing:

> "This is my son in whom I take great delight."
> (see Matthew 12:18)

❖ ❖ ❖

A Prayer to Pray

Father, delight in me. Take what is Yours, what belongs to You. Jesus, come into Your garden. You are my faithful bridegroom, the desire of my heart. Come and take Your fill of me. I don't want to hold anything back, Lord. I declare that unworthiness has no place in my life. Because of Your love, because of Your sacrifice, the blood You shed for me, I am worthy. Take delight in me. Give me a revelation of Your delight, of how pleasing I am to You. Release Your laughter over me; release Your song over me, Lord. Smile on me, Lord. Let the light of Your face shine on me.

CHAPTER 2
The Necessity of the Holy Spirit

BY MATTHEW LOZANO

Many people have come to Christ as the result of my participation in presenting the Gospel to them. It's ALL the work of the Holy Spirit. [Emphasis added] (BILLY GRAHAM)

In reciting the Nicene Creed, the most widely accepted and used statement of faith in the Christian church, we affirm that we "believe in the Holy Spirit, the Lord, the giver of life, who proceeds from the Father and the Son. With the Father and the Son, He is worshiped and glorified. He has spoken through the Prophets." Sadly, the Holy Spirit, co-equal with the Father and the Son, is often ignored. We usually give Jesus the worship due Him; we occasionally give the Father His due worship; we almost never worship and glorify the Spirit. Check out any song list or hymnal and you will see that this is true. It is evident that we often overlook how important our relationship to the Holy Spirit is and how important it is for us to understand Him. Why do we pass over the Holy Spirit? It may be fear; it may be simple misunderstanding; it may be discomfort because of church divisions over the work of the Spirit. My point is this: to ignore the third person of the Trinity is a big mistake. The Holy Spirit is vitally important to our lives, and our relationship to Him is the crucial, essential, primary aspect of the Christian life. Without the Spirit, we could not receive revelation, know Jesus, be His disciple, worship Him, or glorify Him. The role of the Spirit is to show us Jesus. When we neglect the Spirit at work in our lives, our efforts to serve God tend to be man-centered, fruitless, and misguided. When we try to be like Jesus by our own human efforts, it doesn't work.

Jesus Himself told us it wouldn't work without the Spirit. He said, "…it is to your advantage that I go away, for if I do not go away, the Counselor will not come to you; but if I go, I will send Him to you" (John 16:7). I marvel at that statement. It was better for us that Jesus *go away* because of whom He would send to us. Jesus is the image of the invisible God, and He took on flesh to reveal the Father to us. In the fullness of time, Jesus revealed the fullness of the Father's love to us through His life, sacrificial death, and resurrection. God's love could now be seen, heard, and touched. That revelation, however, does not transform our hearts until the Spirit comes to touch our faith. Jesus had to be exalted to His rightful place, the highest place of authority and glory, and *the Spirit had come to live in the hearts of His followers.* The Holy Spirit empowered them—and empowers us—to receive the revelation of Jesus and to live the Christian life out of that revelation.

A Person to Know

One of the most beloved blessings in the Bible is found at the end of Paul's second letter to Corinth: "The grace of the Lord Jesus Christ and the love of God and the fellowship of the Holy Spirit be with you all" (2 Corinthians 13:14). Stop a minute and meditate on that. This is the gospel right there. The love of God the Father is expressed through the grace and peace from Jesus, who is your salvation. You received that grace and responded to it by the power of the Holy Spirit. You can't experience the fullness of the grace and peace that comes from Jesus without the Holy Spirit. You can't experience the love of the Father without the Holy Spirit. But there is more: Paul's benediction doesn't say "getting touched" by the Holy Spirit. He doesn't pray the "anointing of the Holy Spirit be with you all." No, Paul prays for "the fellowship of the Spirit." Sweet, uninterrupted fellowship, like the fellowship of the Trinity itself. Fellowship where you abide with and follow the Spirit. A fellowship where the Spirit rests on you. Do you know what it *really* means to live like Jesus? Do you know from where those amazing teachings, miraculous signs and wonders, compassionate healings, and astounding prophecies flowed? They came through the humanity of Jesus, who dwelt in unbroken fellowship with the Father's heart, and on whom the Spirit rested like a dove.

So let me introduce you to the Holy Spirit. He is a Person. He is not electricity, although His presence may affect you like electricity. He is not merely power, although when He shows up, there is power. He's a Person. You have to understand a person in order to relate to him. As mentioned in the previous chapter, if you want to know a person, you should know his passion, his greatest desire. What is the Holy Spirit's great desire? To glorify Jesus in the human heart, for the praise and glory of the Father.

DIVINE COMMUNICATION: EXPRESSING THE LOVE OF GOD

The essence of God is love. In relation to Himself, God is a family of Persons, a fellowship of eternal love. The Father delights in the Son, pleased with His eternal devotion and unwavering obedience and friendship. The Son revels in His Father's love, always desiring the pleasure of His heart and the service of His will. The Father longs to give the Son an inheritance and a bride, the Church who will love Him forever. The Son longs to reveal the glory of His Father and give everything back to the Father. Close your eyes and try to imagine the dynamic emotional power that is released when the Father and Son look into each other's eyes. Can you imagine what this eternal friendship, intimacy, favor, loyalty, and love might look like? Could such a force be contained?

There is a third Person between the Father and the Son. He is described as the essence of this love between the Father and Son. Whenever there is this expression of love between the Father and the Son, the Holy Spirit bursts forth. When God created the universe as an inheritance for His Son, where was the Holy Spirit, the "Lord, the Giver of Life"? Hovering over the deep. The Holy Spirit is the dynamic power present at creation, the breath of God that formed life. When you came into being, you were an expression of the Father's heart toward His Son. You are a love letter to Jesus, crafted by the Spirit, often referred to as the artist of creation.

This dynamic repeats itself in *every* communication that comes from God. It looks like this: *revelation begins in the heart of the Father, is revealed by the Son, and is expressed by the Holy Spirit* who enables us to receive the revelation. God's love is expressed to His creation, and to the human heart, by the Holy Spirit. Not only did our universe begin by the dynamic (*dunamis*) power of God, but every word of the Bible was inspired by this same power of love. The Holy Spirit, you see, is the self-expression of God. Whenever prophets spoke, the Spirit was present. When Jesus was anointed to announce the reign of His Father (the design of His heart), the Spirit came and rested upon Him. As you read the Scriptures, you will be excited to find Him everywhere. God is speaking!

Jesus is our model for life as sons and daughters of God. He lived in complete surrender. Jesus said two important things about His life: "I only do what My Father is doing," and "My words are Spirit and Life" (see John 5:19 and John 6:63). In other words, Jesus never did anything apart from the will of His Father, and He never *said* a thing but by the Holy Spirit. As the revelation of God to humanity, Jesus shows the way and the truth for us to follow: *it takes God to love God and it takes God to love others*. We are dependent on the Holy Spirit to reveal God's love to us, and we cooperate with Him to express love back to God.

Our Counselor and Helper

Here is why you need the Holy Spirit so much: In 1 Corinthians 12:3, Paul writes that "no one can say 'Jesus is Lord' except by the Holy Spirit." As our confession came by the Spirit, so too all that Jesus commands us will be done as we "keep in step with the Spirit." It takes God to love God.

The good news is that through faith and baptism, the Holy Spirit comes to live in us. What does that mean for us today? The Holy Spirit is the Spirit of truth. He will lead you into all truth. Therefore, if you want the truth about anything in the kingdom, you need the fellowship of the Holy Spirit. He's referred to as the Paraclete, a counselor/lawyer, and He comes to convict the world of sin, of righteousness, and of judgment. Jesus is the revelation of God the Father; the Holy Spirit confirms that revelation. In John 16:14, Jesus said the Holy Spirit "... will glorify Me, for He will take what is Mine and declare it to you." He follows it up by saying "all that the Father has is Mine." Remember, every blessing, every communication from God starts in the heart of the Father, is revealed by the Son, and is communicated through the Holy Spirit. Understand what Jesus is saying. He shares with you all the glory that came to Him by the Holy Spirit. Everything the Father has—the Father's heart of love for Jesus, the Father's blessing—now comes to you through the Holy Spirit. So if you want more of Jesus, ask for the Holy Spirit. If you want more capacity to love like Jesus, ask the Holy Spirit for help. He desires nothing less than to glorify Jesus through you.

Let me give you an example of how the Spirit works. One of our prayer leaders was fatigued at the end of a long conference. Some of the conference attendees brought a woman to her who was experiencing what seemed to be an asthma attack. Although the others wanted to get medical help, *the woman herself* sensed the cause of her shortness of breath was spiritual. So our prayer leader sought the counsel of the Holy Spirit and waited upon Him for wisdom. As she was praying, the woman had a vision of her aunt choking her. It was clear from this image that whatever her aunt had done in the past to her caused her great fear and anxiety. After forgiving her aunt and renouncing the fear, both her anxiety and her shortness of breath were gone. The Spirit enables us to see past the physical reality and cooperate with what God is doing.

The Promised Holy Spirit—He's Bringing Gifts

In his letter to the Ephesians, Paul prays for you "to be strengthened with might through His Spirit in the inner man, [so] that Christ may dwell in your hearts through faith." The Spirit strengthens you to make you a bigger and stronger God-container. Why? Paul's prayer continues by saying, "That you, being rooted and grounded in love, may have power to comprehend with all the saints what is the breadth and length and height and depth, and to know the love of Christ which surpasses knowledge, that you may be filled with all the fullness of

God" (Ephesians 3:16-19). If you want the fullness of God dwelling in you, you must be strengthened by the Holy Spirit.

The Spirit is offered to you generously. In Luke 11, Jesus tells His followers to ask for the Holy Spirit. The Father is not stingy with His Spirit. Jesus says:

> *And I tell you, ask, and it will be given you; seek, and you will find; knock, and it will be opened to you. For every one who asks receives, and he who seeks finds, and to him who knocks it will be opened. What father among you, if his son asks for a fish, will instead of a fish give him a serpent; or if he asks for an egg, will give him a scorpion? If you then, who are evil, know how to give good gifts to your children, how much more will the heavenly Father give the Holy Spirit to those who ask Him!*
>
> Luke 11:9-13

No, He is not stingy. Why? Because the Father knows the way to glorify His Son in creation is to unleash the Holy Spirit. Stand back and watch Him work!

The Spirit has so much to give you. The Spirit in you calls out "Abba, Father." The Spirit enables you to have that *intimate* relationship with the Father. The Spirit comforts you, seals you, and lets you know you have been chosen. Where the Spirit of the Lord is, there is *freedom* as sons and daughters of God (2 Corinthians 3:17). The Spirit brings *unity* among believers. Do you want unity in your church, in your family, in the world? The Spirit brings it. The Holy Spirit is a person who brings all these gifts and more. Paul said we should eagerly desire the gifts He gives (1 Corinthians 14:1). Why? So we can mature.

> *And His gifts were that some should be apostles, some prophets, some evangelists, some pastors and teachers, to equip the saints for the work of ministry, for building up the body of Christ, until we all attain to the unity of the faith and of the knowledge of the Son of God, to mature manhood, to the measure of the stature of the fullness of Christ…"*
>
> Ephesians 4:11-13

You actually help others grow to spiritual maturity by using the gifts the Spirit gives you. What are these gifts, these manifestations?

They are the message of wisdom, knowledge, faith, healing, miracles, prophecy, discernment, speaking of tongues, the interpretation of tongues, strengthening, encouragement, comfort, teaching, and administration, among others. How many of you have recognized the manifestation of the Holy Spirit in *administration*? Wow! He's a far better giver than Santa Claus. Wherever and whenever you see the Holy Spirit at work in you or your fellow believer, honor it as you would a gift from a person. Celebrate His actions in your own life and in the lives of those around you and you will be celebrating Him. Eagerly desire and cultivate respect for the Holy Spirit's gifts. Don't judge any fellowship or believer by the externals. Instead, witness to the glorious work of the dynamic power of God unleashed by the Spirit in them. Since the Spirit is the finger of God, an artist whose medium is people, this honors Him. We are His masterpiece when we reflect the unity and love of our Maker.

Delicious Fruit

The Spirit produces something in you. Fruit. Do you like fruit? I love fruit. Strawberries, papaya, pineapple—fruit is so delicious. *Delightful.* You know Jesus likes to produce good fruit in us, don't you? Look at what He did to the fig tree when it wasn't producing good fruit (see Mark 11:12-14). He loves good fruit. The Spirit produces fruit in you for Jesus to enjoy—peace, patience, kindness, goodness, faithfulness, gentleness, and self-control. These are manifestations of the Holy Spirit, expressions of love toward your Savior—God manifesting His love in your life. And they are *pleasing* to Jesus. If you want to be pleasing to Jesus, pay attention not only to your actions; pay attention to the fruit that is produced as you are in fellowship with the Holy Spirit.

Fruit comes as you keep in step with the Spirit. Paul says you have a choice to live either by the Spirit or by the sinful nature: "But I say, walk by the Spirit, and do not gratify the desires of the flesh. For the desires of the flesh are against the Spirit, and the desires of the Spirit are against the flesh; for these are opposed to each other, to prevent you from doing what you would. But if you are led by the Spirit you are not under the law" (Galatians 5:16-18).

The Holy Spirit is so single-minded, so undivided in His love and in His passionate pursuit to see Jesus glorified that you cannot live by the Spirit and by the sinful nature at the same time. You can't. So keep in step with the Spirit. Stay in fellowship with the Holy Spirit. If we rely on ourselves to wrestle with our sinful nature, we too often ignore the counsel of the Spirit.

Power Comes Through Filling

The Spirit empowers you to be His witness. Just before His ascension to His Father, Jesus told His disciples, "All authority in heaven and on earth has been given to Me." He took His authority and passed it on to His followers, telling them to go throughout the world and bring others to Him. But before they could go, they had to wait for the gift of the Holy Spirit. Why? Because they needed His power: "But you shall receive power when the Holy Spirit has come upon you; and you shall be My witnesses in Jerusalem and in all Judea and Sama'ria and to the end of the earth" (Acts 1:8). You see? It takes God to love God, and it takes the Spirit to enable you to be a witness, to give you power. Jesus gives you His authority, but the Holy Spirit gives you the power. The work of God can only be done in the power and strength of God.

So the Spirit dwells in you. Paul says you need to be "filled" with the Holy Spirit. Are you full? Are you filled with the Holy Spirit? Or are you getting in the way of the Spirit? Are you getting in the way of the Holy Spirit in His effort to glorify Jesus in your life? Are you trying to glorify Jesus on your own? Do you need to step aside? Do you need to be introduced to the Spirit? Say, "Welcome, Holy Spirit. Come and do what You do best. Come and glorify Jesus in my heart. Take what belongs to Jesus and reveal it to me. Change my heart. Strengthen me to be a bigger container for God. Strengthen me so Christ can dwell in my heart through faith."

John the Baptist said Jesus would baptize you with the Holy Spirit and with fire. Jesus came to pave the way to the Father and then send the Spirit that you might become like Jesus for the glory of God. Do you want the Holy Spirit a little bit? Do you just want goose bumps? Or do you want unbroken fellowship with the Holy Spirit in which Jesus is completely glorified and the Spirit rests on you? The third Person of the Godhead desires a relationship with you. It is in this relationship that power is released to expose the darkness and bring liberty to the oppressed. "Where the Spirit of the Lord is there is freedom" (2 Corinthians 3:17).

* * *

A Prayer to Pray

Come, Holy Spirit. Spirit of God, who created life, You are the Lord and giver of life. You burst forth from the Trinity as the very expression of God, the dynamic power of God, the lover of Jesus in human hearts, and I want to welcome You. Holy Spirit, forgive me for the ways I've treated You like a thing. Forgive me for the ways I've tried to follow Jesus on my own and neglected Your counsel, Your comfort, and Your wisdom. I repent of the ways I've neglected to keep in step with You. Rid me of darkness; rid me of the things that hold me back. Cleanse me so fear will have no place in a heart that is loved.

Reveal Jesus to me, I pray, in a deeper way. Enlarge my heart that I might receive more of God. I honor You because You are the best at glorifying Jesus. You are the best at bringing out praise and glory. You are the best at taking what is God's and revealing it to my heart. Have Your way with me. Clothe me with Your power. Holy Spirit move in my heart today that I would be transformed, that You would produce good fruit in me. Make me a radiant lover of Jesus, a heartfelt responder to the love of God, and a faithful and beloved child who moves boldly to You. To please You is my greatest desire.

Release Your gifts in me, Lord. Give me the grace to listen deeply to others and to speak to others in psalms and spiritual hymns, to bless, to encourage, and to use the gifts you give me to set the captives free. Holy Spirit, I ask for unbroken fellowship with You. Come and descend on me today. Amen.

CHAPTER 3

Humility: The Nature of Christ

Come to Me, all who labor and are heavy laden, and I will give you rest. Take My yoke upon you, and learn from Me; for I am gentle and lowly in heart, and you will find rest for your souls. (MATTHEW 11:28-29)

Jim serves on the prayer ministry at his church. When the pastor calls for the prayer team to come forward, Jim leaves his seat and calmly walks to the front. He is pleased to be recognized as a leader in prayer. He knows the congregation is watching. He remains solemn. He turns to face the congregation and waits to serve someone in prayer. A woman comes up and goes left to a prayer minister on the other side of the church. A man comes up and draws away the prayer minister standing next to Jim. Jim shuffles his feet. Why did no one ask him to pray? He is the only prayer team member left.

The congregation comes to the end of the last song and Jim feels like his ministry is rejected today. Just as the pastor begins his benediction, a second woman comes up, one who asks for prayer every Sunday; she comes to him. Jim finds her irritating and is usually eager to look busy with another parishioner, but today he is relieved to have someone standing in front of him. He prays for her quickly. The pastor catches him by the arm as he walks down the aisle.

"Thank you for your willingness to serve by praying with people."

Jim smiles. His chest expands a bit as warm satisfaction fills him.

Jim is serving out of his fallen nature, the nature of Adam and Eve that grasps at equality with God. Left to ourselves, the fallen nature is all we would know. But Jesus came to provide a way of escape from pride and rebellion. He offers us His character, His nature, and invites us to make an exchange: our nature for His. He tells us He is "gentle and lowly in heart" (Matthew 11:29). Because of His death and resurrection, you now have a choice to either follow the old fallen nature of a son or daughter of Adam or become like Him—the second Adam—in His humility.

> *Do nothing from selfishness or conceit, but in humility count others better than yourselves. Let each of you look not only to his own interests, but also to the interests of others. Have this mind among yourselves, which is yours in Christ Jesus, who, though He was in the form of God, did not count equality with God a thing to be grasped, but emptied Himself, taking the form of a servant, being born in the likeness of men. And being found in human form He humbled Himself and became obedient unto death, even death on a cross."*
>
> Philippians 2:3-8

Jesus invites the multitudes to come and find rest. He communicates that invitation through you as you also are gentle and lowly in heart. Does this frighten you? It should not, for humility is not beyond your grasp. Remember the words of Paul in Galatians 2:20: "I have been crucified with Christ; it is no longer I who live, but Christ who lives in me; and the life I now live in the flesh I live by faith in the Son of God, who loved me and gave Himself for me." Jesus lives in you. Jesus lives through you. As you keep in step with His Spirit, you can have His mind and grow in His character. In the Holy Spirit's power, you can empty yourself and serve as your Master served: without fear. You can be assured that in humbling yourself, you will lose nothing. For as the Scriptures say, "Humble yourselves before the Lord and He will exalt you" (James 4:10).

Building on the One Foundation

Paul tells us all our works for the kingdom will be tested by fire. If we have built with gold, silver, and precious stones, our works will last, but anything built with wood, hay, or straw will burn (1 Corinthians 3). You will want to build well to please the Lord and for the sake of those who come for ministry. Humbly binding yourself to the character of Christ ensures your works are indeed gold. Humility, then, is your guarantee that your works will last and receive a reward, for Scripture says, "For no other foundation can anyone lay than that which is laid, which is Jesus Christ (1 Corinthians 3:11). The humility of Christ provides the pathway for people in need to find their way to the Father's house.

Jesus served in humility. On the night before He died, Jesus "rose from supper, laid aside His garments, and girded Himself with a towel. Then He poured water into a basin, and began to wash the disciples' feet, and to wipe them with the towel with which He was girded" (John 13: 4-5). This gospel account should leave an indelible image in your mind: Jesus, the Son of Almighty God, washing feet. I cannot imagine the disciples would ever have forgotten the moment Jesus touched their feet and washed them. For some of them, this may have been the last time Jesus physically touched them before His death. They remembered His words: "you also ought to wash one another's feet" (John 13:14). And the promise made that night to them belongs now to you: "If you know these things and do them, you will be blessed" (John 13:17, paraphrased).

Every time we present UNBOUND training, we repeat the following: "Our job is not to set the captive free; that is the Lord's job. Our job is to love and accept the person while using the Five Keys to listen and assist him." When someone comes to you for prayer, you are there to wash feet, to touch him or her with God's love, and to serve. The five keys are like the basin and towel; you will be like Jesus, who rose from His place and lowered Himself to serve as one who is sent. Every time you minister to someone using the Five Keys, you have an opportunity to lean deeper into true humility. As you witness the work of the Savior setting captives free, there is little room to exalt yourself but plenty of room to sing the praises of God. We serve, knowing that our need to receive will come again as God pursues us and draws us to deeper freedom. We are like those we serve.

GOING LOWER

In order to successfully build a ministry, or a lifetime of personal service, humility must be your foundation. St. Augustine understood that well, often emphasizing humility as foundational. In a sermon on Matthew 19:28, he says, "Do you wish to be great? Begin from the least. Are you thinking of constructing a high and mighty fabric? Think first of the foundation of humility. The greater you wish your building to be, the deeper must be its foundation. The building, in the course of its construction, rises up on high, but he who digs its foundation must first go down very low. So you can see that even a building is low before it is high, and the top is raised only after bowing down."[1]

If your ministry is characterized by humility, it will reveal the kingdom. If ministry is not done out of humility, it will fail when tested by fire. Without humility, there is no love. Without love, you are only "a noisy gong or a clanging cymbal…I am nothing…I gain nothing" (see 1 Corinthians 13:1-3). Augustine is said to have explained it this way: "Humility is the foundation of all the other virtues: hence, in the soul in which this virtue does not exist there cannot be any other virtue except in mere appearance." As you learn to minister using the Five Keys, you will see how serving in humility is interwoven throughout the guidelines we provide. As you study and as you serve, you are invited to "put on" humility.

In the Scriptures we are told to "put on…lowliness" (Colossians 3:12), "humble yourselves" (1 Peter 5:6), "clothe yourselves…with humility" (1 Peter 5:5), and "go and sit in the lowest place" (see Luke 14: 7-11). In Luke 18: 9-14, Jesus makes it clear it is the humble tax collector, rather than the pompous Pharisee, who leaves his prayer time right with God. Your acts of humility, united to Him by faith, become a doorway for the presence of real humility. Humility is a gift that is found in union with the One who emptied Himself, endured the shame and suffering of the cross, washed you of your sins by His very blood, and restored you to the Father. When you take the opportunity to walk in this gift, even if only for a moment, you will know your humility is not a product of your efforts but a grace that visits you. The moment you begin to serve by your own power, this grace may be lifted. Guard the gift of humility by practicing it daily.

---

[1] St. Augustine, paraphrased from *Sermons on Selected Lessons of the New Testament* (Grand Rapids: Eerdmans, 1994; reprint of 1887 book), 664.

Truth Expressed in Humility

Humility is simply the truth about who God is and who you are. Humility is being secure in God's love and His favor toward you. G. K. Chesterton said, "It is always the secure who are humble."[2] Humility and security go together just as pride and insecurity (fear) are interwoven. Pride will lead you to believe you need to save yourself (justify yourself) and that life is fullest when you are the center. Humility recognizes you are always safe in the hands of God and that life is most delightful when you can serve from the heart, trusting Him. The pathway of pride is a pathway to loneliness and isolation. The pathway of humility is a pathway to companionship and honor.

We all battle with pride and insecurity. Any efforts to serve humbly will expose the enemy and reveal the battle within. Let me share some typical symptoms:

- You decide to serve, to take the last place, but find yourself compulsively wondering whether anyone notices how you are serving.

- When you are thanked for your service, you feed off the words as if you were starving. You collect a few crumbs but are not satisfied.

- You compare yourself to others, evaluating your standing before God and others. Insecurity drives you to say, "Do I deserve God's love?" or "I know that I am better than she," or "I am not as good as he."

Have you ever admired certain parents whose children seem free to be themselves yet so obedient and respectful at the same time? I know families like this. Getting a glimpse of these blessings can give you a sense of awe. If you were to express to them your admiration, they might say "thank you" and smile (saying thanks is an expression of humility). Inwardly they might think, "If you only knew what goes on every day at our house"—and then whisper thanks to God for they know He is the one behind every good thing. They know every blessing

---

[2] G. K. Chesterton, *On Lying in Bed and Other Essays* (Calgary, Alberta: Bayeux Arts, Inc., 2000), 365.

comes from God. This knowledge of the bigger reality, this acknowledgement of the truth, is true humility. You do not gain humility by denying your part or minimizing your abilities. No, you find humility by maximizing your awareness of the grace and action of God, who makes all things possible for those who believe.

Humility does not dwell on what has been accomplished. It is good to take great pleasure in helping another toward freedom in Christ, but the pleasure should be wrapped in the blanket of gratitude and praise to God for what He has done. The greater pleasure is in knowing Him who once again showed Himself as merciful, faithful, and loving. The joy you have in the service you have given or the work you have done is really the pleasure of having fellowship with the Lord, who has led you and empowered you. God does not dwell in the past. You can draw from the past visitations of the Lord to enkindle your trust in Him today. God has made His home in you and He dwells in it today. If you retire and seek to live off past victories, you will dry up like an old well. The well will remind you of the water, but there will be none to draw from. Like the manna in the desert, the nourishment is only for a day. Today's water, today's bread is found in staying focused on the mission the Lord has graciously given you: to go lower as you continue to serve His people.

Growing in Humility

If God has called you to help others find freedom in Christ, you want to have your work count in His kingdom. How will you grow in humility when your natural instincts and the call of the world are bent toward pride? Here are my suggestions:

1. *Recognize that humility is, above all, the work of God.*

Many spiritual disciplines help us to enter into the truth. But I do not know any that is as effective as God's own work through your life's circumstances. As you seek to live in the truth as a disciple of Jesus, your pride will be exposed and the grace of humiliation will bring you into humility. When you face the trials of life, God will work humility into you as you cling to the truth. When you are truly humble, you will be surprised; it will not occur to you to boast of your humility because you know this gift mysteriously appeared from the hand of God.

As a Pharisee, Paul wanted to serve God and he served with zeal. But when he was knocked to the ground on the Damascus road, blinded so that he had to shuffle with his hands in front of him, humiliated in front of his companions, he was on the way to learning humility. He heard the voice of the Lord saying "Saul, Saul, why do you persecute Me?" And then, "I am Jesus, whom you are persecuting." Saul recognized the truth. If we resist the One whom we have called Lord and God, we will surely find humiliation—and through it an opportunity to receive the gift of humility.

2. *Practice submitting to authorities in your life.*

All of us are under authority, but sometimes we don't want to submit. If—unlike the Roman centurion who told Jesus, "I am unworthy... But say the word and my servant will be healed" (Luke 7)—you insist you know better, you are right, or you deserve appreciation in your human relationships, you may find yourself doing the same thing with God. The apostle Peter presents you with both an invitation and a warning when he says, "Likewise you that are younger be subject to the elders. Clothe yourselves, all of you, with humility toward one another, for 'God opposes the proud, but gives grace to the humble'" (1 Peter 5:5). Let people encounter you as one who is dressed in humility, for you can be assured of this: God will oppose you in your pride; He loves you too much to leave you bound by it.

3. *Yield to humility.*

One of my first lessons in humility came many years ago. I remember there was a group of people praying with me. When I prayed aloud, it was as if I was listening to another person. I heard in my prayer an expression of real humility. It did not sound like me! The Holy Spirit inspired the prayer. As you yield to Jesus, who advances the kingdom through you, you can yield to the humility He is working in you.

4. *Embrace your weakness.*

It has been said we should not waste a good crisis. This is true of the Apostle Paul. He suffered humiliations all to his advantage. God's power was made perfect in weakness. Paul writes:

> *But He said to me, "My grace is sufficient for you, for My power is made perfect in weakness." I will all the more gladly boast of my weaknesses, that the power of Christ may rest upon me. For the sake of Christ, then, I am content with weaknesses, insults, hardships, persecutions, and calamities; for when I am weak, then I am strong.*
>
> 2 Corinthians 12:9-10

When weaknesses, insults, hardships, persecutions, and calamities come your way, you need to battle to trust in God's grace and be content, knowing there is a greater work going on in you that will enable you to serve as Jesus served.

5. *Identify false humility.*

False humility plagues the people of God. When the Scriptures say, "In humility count others better than yourselves" (Philippians 2:3), this does not mean the other person is more worthy than you, loved by God in a greater way, or more deserving. It simply means you ought to consider another as having a higher position, someone whom you have the opportunity to serve. Jesus had no trouble saying the Father was greater than He was. He honored the Father as one whom He loved, served, and obeyed, yet He was co-equal with God. False humility rejects the honor others would give you, not out of true "sober judgment" but out of a pride that refuses to accept what God and others say about you. C.S. Lewis points out that a truly humble man is not at all the one who puts himself down:

> Do not imagine that if you meet a really humble man he will be what most people call "humble" nowadays: he will not be a sort of greasy, smarmy person, who is always telling you that, of course, he is nobody. Probably all you will think about him is that he seemed a cheerful, intelligent chap who took a real interest in what *you* said to *him*. If you do dislike him it will be because you feel a little envious of anyone who seems to enjoy life so easily. He will not be thinking about humility: he will not be thinking about himself at all.[3]

---

[3] C. S. Lewis, *Mere Christianity* (New York: Macmillan, 1960), 114.

6. *Remember the victory.*

In Christ, you have died and risen to a new life. In Him, you are dead to the past sins and shameful ways. When you sin and confess that sin, God takes the sin as far as the east is from the west and remembers it no more (Psalm 103:12). False humility leads you back to your sin. Pride prevents you from moving on. Follow the example Paul gives to Timothy when he says the following:

> *Though I formerly blasphemed and persecuted and insulted Him; but I received mercy because I had acted ignorantly in unbelief, and the grace of our Lord overflowed for me with the faith and love that are in Christ Jesus. The saying is sure and worthy of full acceptance, that Christ Jesus came into the world to save sinners. And I am the foremost of sinners.*
>
> 1 Timothy 1:13-15

Paul could recall his sins and even declare he was the greatest of sinners, but he did it for one reason: to demonstrate the greater truth that Christ came into this world to save sinners. He understood that with greater awareness of sin comes greater appreciation for what God has done through His Son. When you are tempted to go back to your sins and condemn yourself, you need to recognize the pit from where that condemnation comes. And, like Paul, turn the condemnation back on your enemy by giving thanks and praise for your Savior who delivered you from ignorance and unbelief, and revealed the mercy of God. In humility, accept that in Christ Jesus you have been forgiven and justified and are, every day, being conformed to His image.

7. *Take your stand against the devil's schemes.*

UNBOUND ministry exposes the deceitful tactics of the devil, his lies, and his hidden influence. As you use the Five Keys to help someone else, you may see things in your own life that need to be brought under the Lord's authority. Humble yourself before God and take your stand against your enemy. Every ministry session is a chance for God to do more work in you.

You may be thinking right now that you are not very humble. Be assured that the virtue of humility grows over time as you follow the Lord. If you ask God for humility, I can promise you God will respond. I have never known that prayer to fail anyone! If you ask, an opportunity to humble yourself is on its way. Chances are, as you are a follower of Jesus, it is already on its way and your prayer will help you to recognize it not simply as the devil's attack but as an opportunity to yield to the grace of humility. Do not be deceived. Not all opposition is from the devil; not every battle is the enemy on the loose. Remember, God opposes the proud but gives grace to the humble.

"Pride ends in humiliation, while humility brings honor" (Proverbs 29:23 NLT).

✢ ✢ ✢

A Prayer to Pray

Father, show me Your glory. Let me stand in Your presence so I will really know who I am. Let me taste Your greatness, Lord. I repent of trusting in myself and in my own abilities. I repent of comparing myself to others. Show me how I put myself first and cling to my self-made identity. Lord Jesus, I surrender my heart and all my circumstances to You. Please release a greater measure of Your Spirit in me. I want to be like Jesus, who is meek and humble of heart.

CHAPTER 4
Compassion: The Heart of Christ

Intense Love does not measure; it just gives. (MOTHER TERESA)

"If I were lying on the couch with a 105-degree temperature," said one woman, "and someone came to my door asking for UNBOUND ministry, I would jump off the couch with delight at the opportunity to serve." What motivates her? What motivates my seventy-five-year-old friend, who now has to let go of the ministries he has participated in for years, to say, "I can't stop doing UNBOUND." What moves *you* to listen to painful and sometimes horrifying stories? Is it the joy at seeing the Lord work? Is it generosity? Is it love? It may be all of those, but underneath, forming the bedrock for joy and generosity, is the first article of "clothing" we are instructed to put on: compassion. "Put on then, as God's chosen ones, holy and beloved, compassion, kindness, lowliness, meekness, and patience" (Colossians 3:12). When we are clothed with compassion, we have tapped into an aspect of God's love that has found a home deep within our being and now flows out from its very depths.

THE GOD OF COMPASSION

The King James Version of the Bible translates *compassion* as "bowels of mercies." The bowels were understood to be the seat of the warm, tender emotions and feelings. To have compassion, then, is to feel with (and for) others, to touch their pain, to know it, to experience it, and to enter into it. As followers of Christ, we are called to enter into another's suffering. Why? Because the God of revelation enters into our suffering. He is the God of compassion. When the Lord revealed Himself to Moses, He defined His name and His character as compassionate and gracious, a God of mercy and forgiveness.

> *Then the LORD came down in the cloud and stood there with him and proclaimed His name, the LORD. And He passed in front of Moses, proclaiming, "The LORD, the LORD, the compassionate and gracious God, slow to anger, abounding in love and faithfulness, maintaining love to thousands, and forgiving wickedness, rebellion and sin. Yet He does not leave the guilty unpunished; He punishes the children and their children for the sin of the fathers to the third and fourth generation."*
> Exodus 34:5-7 (NIV)

He is not only a God who is righteous, hates sin, and judges those who hide under sin's cloak. God knows our pain. He is a God who hears our cries: "Then the LORD said, 'I have seen the affliction of My people who are in Egypt, and have heard their cry because of their taskmasters; I know their suffering'" (Exodus 3:7).

God did not simply satisfy the legal requirement by sending His Son to die for us; He sent His Son to become one of us. The God of compassion and justice has made it known to anyone who would look upon the crucified Christ that He knows our suffering. Jesus, who knew no sin, learned obedience by suffering. He experienced all our emotions; He even experienced our sin through His identification with us and our sin. He experienced sin's devastating consequence at Calvary. He went to the heart of the human condition of sin and separation and experienced, on the cross, our sense of abandonment. He experienced all this because, when He looked on us, He was moved by compassion.

THE HEART OF THE FATHER

Jesus is the heart of the Father revealed to us. He knew the Father as no one else could. When Jesus told a story about the Father, He spoke of a father whose heart was broken over his two lost sons (Luke 15). His own heart was broken by His lost city, Jerusalem. His own heart was broken by those lost under their darkened minds. And so Jesus Christ was moved by compassion. Because compassion is love in *action*, He was moved to heal the sick (Matthew 14:14), give sight to the blind (Matthew 20:34), feed the hungry (Mark 8:2), and teach those who were like sheep without a shepherd (Mark 6:34). He was even moved by compassion to raise the dead (Luke 7:13). And when He described the love of the father for his lost prodigal son, He said, "His father saw him and had compassion, and ran and embraced him and kissed him" (Luke 15:20). In everything He did, Jesus was the "light penetrating darkness" (see John 1:5). He is still the light penetrating the darkness of the human heart, still the lover whose heart is broken for His people living in the darkness of sin, trauma, abuse, deception, rejection, and abandonment.

On several occasions, I have experienced the intensity of His broken heart. These are graced moments I will never forget. On one occasion, I was praying with members of my community for another community that, unbeknownst to us, was about to go through a painful split. As we prayed, we experienced a sense of God's agony; we were filled with an understanding of God's broken heart. Tears streamed down our faces as we felt God's heart in a way that cannot be described with words. As I think about that time, I cannot help but think of Romans 8:26: "Likewise the Spirit helps us in our weakness; for we do not know how to pray as we ought, but the Spirit Himself intercedes for us with sighs too deep for words." We did not have an understanding of what was going to happen, but we knew the intensity of God's compassion for our friends. This was one of the most profound moments of my life.

My second encounter with the Lord's broken heart occurred overseas. In the middle of talking to leaders of an evangelization movement, I began to weep and sob. If I had not sensed it was God's heart being expressed, I would have been humiliated by the expression of emotion and by my inability to speak. Months later, they too went through a painful split.

From these experiences, I learned first that no matter what trouble or tragedy or pain you go through, the Lord has seen it. He knows your pain before you feel it and He has interceded for you before the Father. He has wept over you. I learned secondly that His compassion and His desire to save are overwhelmingly deep. Once, as I prayed, God allowed me to participate in His intercession—the intercession flowing from the broken heart of God. I found myself repeating, "Lord, save Your people. Save Your people." Afterward, I wondered why I was praying for His people and not for the lost. Now, years later, as I bring a message of freedom to God's people, I understand what God was doing in me and who He has made me to be. If you have never had an experience like this in prayer, you may not understand that God's heart is full of joy at the same time that it is broken. When intercession is released, He can restore you in a moment and fill your heart with joy. The pain you feel does not linger, for it is not your pain. It is His love finding expression in you.

Compassion flows out of the love and mercy of God in our deepest souls as surely as lava flows from the deepest roots of a volcano. It is a gift of the Holy Spirit. Compassion motivates UNBOUND ministry. If there are less godly desires that motivate you, you must put on kindness, lowliness, meekness, and patience to go with the compassion. Let the Lord humble you more deeply. Repent more completely, but do not fail to recognize that God releases His compassion in you as a gift. Thank Him for the privilege of carrying this treasure. Ask Him to enlarge your heart of compassion; look for opportunities to yield to it so you may release His mercies on those He sends to you.

COMPASSION RELEASED

God, the Father of mercies and comfort, has released compassion into this world through His Son and now through you.

> *Blessed be the God and Father of our Lord Jesus Christ, the Father of mercies and God of all comfort, who comforts us in all our affliction, so that we may be able to comfort those who are in any affliction, with the comfort with which we ourselves are comforted by God.*
>
> 2 Corinthians 1:3-4

His compassion is released in you through your place of pain. Pain is common to all humanity, but each individual deals with pain differently. When you submit to Jesus as the Lord of your life, you (perhaps unknowingly) invite Him into your secret places of hidden pain, pain you would rather ignore, deny, or hide from—painful places that in the past have been overwhelming to you. Perhaps you have learned to manage your pain but not overcome it. If you refuse to be in touch with the realities of the past and close the door to the work of the Spirit to transform you from within, you will minister the Five Keys from a superficial place, a place of knowledge but not of knowing. But when you say yes to Jesus from the place where pain has been touched by God's love, compassion is born in you.

Compassion Trusts

On occasion, people will come to you whom you cannot help. If insecurity, the need to control, or the fear of failure grips your heart, you may fall into trying too hard. Your own efforts leave you vulnerable to fear and worry. The person before you is sent by God for you to love. Only God can set a person free. Never be deceived. Even if you use the Five Keys and miracles happen, it is not because of what you have done. God was at work in the heart of the person long before you met him. Others have sown, and it just "happens" that you are there on the day of reaping.

If someone leaves and he is not set free, believe in the Lord's love for him. Sometimes I find myself wondering about someone I recently prayed for. Will he continue to take hold of his freedom? Will he use the Five Keys to go deeper? Will he go through whatever door God opens next? Will he find a body of believers who will love him? Will he find his purpose and mission? Will he do what is necessary to break out of his isolation? Or, I may reflect, "How could I have better served this person? Did I give him enough counsel as he left or did I give him too much? Oh, I missed something—I wonder if that will be a problem for him. Did God really set him free?" What is the line between compassion and worry?

One man I prayed with left saying he felt twenty pounds lighter. But I wondered. He was becoming an alcoholic. His lifestyle was destroying his marriage. I wondered how much really happened for him during our session. Weeks later, I found out. The man no longer felt addicted to alcohol. He no longer awoke each morning thinking about his next drink. Now he woke with a clear mind. He was no longer depressed and desperate but hopeful. "The "noise" in his head had stopped. He reported, "I no longer have dreams about falling. I am walking on the earth. I feel a burning desire for Christ." Still, I wondered. Would he return to church? Would he stop drinking or would this become a fading memory if he continued to drink, thinking he was no longer in bondage? I know well that the Scripture says, "Pride comes before the fall." Did we deal with the pride? Would he need to be broken again to come back to the Lord?

Some of these thoughts are temptations to worry or control. Though I have these thoughts a lot less than I used to, I am still tempted, sometimes, to worry. You will be too. Temptations always come with a mixture of truth and lie. Many of these thoughts are reasonable. But do they arise from compassion or worry? How do you tell the difference?

Compassion will drive you to pray for each individual who comes to your mind. Worry will keep you thinking about yourself, fretting over your own reputation and fear of failure. As the Lord teaches you to know His heart, you will understand your own heart better. Ask the Lord for revelation and be assured the Master will impart wisdom to you as He teaches you the lessons of life. After any ministry session, yes, ask the Lord to show you how you might have better served the one who sought ministry. Yes, seek to learn every time you minister to someone. Yes, pray for him. No, do not worry. Remember that your job is to simply love the one who came for prayer and use the keys that have been entrusted to you.

Compassion Invites—and Waits

Most people who come to us for prayer are not under our continued care. We simply help them to the breakthrough they need to move on with God. They know they are oppressed; they know something holds them back from becoming the person they could be. They want to be set free and we want them to leave with the freedom to choose to be a disciple of Jesus. We want them to know the joy of following the Master and yielding to the life of the Son of God that has been given to them, but they have been making decisions to accept or reject the grace of God at work in them for years. Some are ready to be set free and some are not. Those who are not ready for freedom need your compassion as much as those who are ready to surrender.

I remember one woman who was not ready. She had come for prayer at the urging of her friend who counseled her and was praying for her healing. She had few other motivations. During the interview, it became obvious she was not taking responsibility for her freedom but wanted to leave it with her friend, with me, and even with God. She wanted God to just go ahead and heal her. God does not work that way. He draws us into the process. Unfortunately, this woman was not ready to fight. She was not willing to renounce the lies that imprisoned her, to trust the Father, and to embrace her new identity in Christ. Though she had a very tender heart, one that drew many people to love her, her old identity was too much a trusted friend to give up. She was too comfortable hiding behind and finding safety in her old self. It was too much of a risk for her to trust in the Lord that day.

Because I sensed this, I reminded her several times that she could end the session any time. I hoped that if I undercut the sense of false safety gained from letting others make her decisions, she would decide to go for freedom in Christ. But once it became evident she wanted to take the open exit door, I let her go. It was difficult, especially since I believed she was so close to freedom. In her case, however, compassion demanded I listen to where she was and allow her to go. She was not ready.

Remember that as powerful as an UNBOUND session is, it is only a part of the bigger work of God's redeeming power in others' lives. God has been at work in them before they came and He will continue to work in them after they leave your ministry. In UNBOUND ministry, you can only do what the Father is doing. So, in every way, respect the person and trust the work of the Holy Spirit in their heart. That is compassion. Yes, you help people take their power back, but you cannot do it for them. You can only do it with them. First Corinthians 13:7-8a tells us "Love bears all things, believes all things, hopes all things, endures all things. Love never ends." Love never fails. If there is one thing I want to impart to you in this chapter, it is that compassion is the love of Christ offered to others through you. And since it is love, compassion does not give up on anyone.

Five months after her initial visit, I got an email from the woman who had not been ready. She wrote, "I realize I was not ready then, but I am ready now." I connected her to some people we had trained for ministry. A few months later, I received another email: "Just wanted to wish you a very Merry Christmas. Thank you for your help this past year; I'm still seeing changes six and seven months after deliverance. If you're ever back in (my state), I owe you a hug." And she attached an emoticon! Now that was a great Christmas present.

You see? Place your confidence in God, do what He has given you to do with love, and trust Him. Carry only the burdens God has given you to carry. If someone is not ready, let them go. Even when someone has received freedom during a prayer session, compassion may bring them to mind in later weeks and months. When you think of them, pray for them, and when you are finished praying, exercise your faith by trusting God and praising Him for His love and mercy; and if you feel led, call them. Remember that He is God and you are not.

COMPASSION AT WORK

I would like to end with a story of compassion. Heidi Baker, a missionary with her husband in Mozambique, has been called the "Protestant Mother Teresa" for her extraordinary work among the poor in her country. In her book *Compelled by Love*, she recounts an earlier time in her life. As you read, consider the perseverance of compassion, the fearlessness of compassion, and the extraordinary power of compassion.

> My great joy is to preach in the villages and streets with alcoholics, the mentally ill, the poor, the outcasts, and the abandoned. Many of these people have great anger issues from lives full of tremendous pain.
>
> I met a girl while preaching on the streets of London. To tell you this story, I will call her Jane. She was so angry that she basically hated everyone, especially men. She had been gang-raped by sixteen men. She had to stay in the hospital for nearly a year with complications from a broken pelvis, and she had no family or friends. She was tormented by hatred and demons, but I loved Jane.
>
> When I met Jane on the streets, she was in her late twenties. Her hair was very short, and she was wearing men's dress shoes and a man's dark suit that was several sizes too big. It took me a while to realize she was a woman. She had a stern, agitated appearance and was full of rage. She could not stand still even for a minute.

I also made another friend—I will call him Peter. Almost every single day for several years, I would go talk to Peter and bring him food. He would yell and tell me to go away and curse at me. He did this for two and a half years. With each curse, I thought how much this man needed love, kindness, and mercy.

I kept bringing Peter potatoes and sandwiches. I refused to stop. Jesus is tenacious: He never stops loving, and he never stops giving. I just kept saying, "I love you, Peter, and Jesus loves you." Sometimes Peter would take the food; other times he would spit at me and throw it on the ground. But God's heart is relentless, and His radical love transforms the hardest of hearts.

One night Jane was so angry, she tried to beat me to death. She told me she would slit my throat with a broken bottle that she was holding and throw me into the Thames River to die. When she tried to strangle me, all I could feel was the pain and suffering in her heart. I felt God's heart for her.

I tried to tell her, "God is in love with you. You are precious. You are called to know His love." This made her angrier!

Then Peter, who had been watching me get beaten the whole time, said he was calling the police. I told him the Lord did not want me to call them. Jane had already been thrown in jail many times and I did not want her to suffer anymore. I wanted her to know the love of Jesus.

Peter just screamed and cursed me again.

Jane had broken the bottle and she said she was going to rip open my face. I kept telling her again how beautiful she was and that I loved her. When I could not feel anything else, I remember praying, "God, whatever You want to do, I just want Your love to be known here."

I felt so tired; I could not take any more pain. I told Jane, "If you are going to kill me, you can just kill me. But I have to sit down."

Just as I prayed, Peter came and rescued me. He grabbed me away from Jane, started sobbing, and then he said, "For two years you told me Jesus loved me. Now I've seen His love, and I want Him. I want Him now. You kept telling me about love, but today I have seen love."

That night Peter fell to his knees and received Jesus as his Lord. We just held each other. Even in his alcoholic state, I just held him and thanked him for saving my life.

We lay our lives down for love, and we give our lives away. We cannot just love with our words. Love is in truth and in our actions.

The following week, Jane came to my house with a dozen roses for me, and she told me that she was sorry for trying to kill me. That day she asked Jesus to live in her heart too.[1]

Reading about Heidi Baker or the life of Mother Teresa reminds me of how God's compassion is not something that is released only in those special moments (like UNBOUND ministry); we are invited to live more deeply as vessels of His compassion every moment of every day. We are to be looking for opportunities to release God's compassion as Mother Teresa did when she went into the streets of Calcutta and looked for the dying so she could serve them. We are to be sensitive to the Holy Spirit, expecting that God will send someone in need to us so His compassion can be released.

Recently I went to a conference with a man who has been used all over the world to proclaim the kingdom and heal the sick. I knew him fairly well twenty years ago. This time, when he greeted me, I was really affected by his love. My eyes were opened to see how he had transformed from a man who loved people to a man consumed with compassion and love. Now more than ever I could see what was motivating him. It was not just his gifting or even the call of God on his life; it was not just a general love but compassion for the one in need standing before him. Compassion is released when it is directed to a person in need.

Compassion is an expression of the love of Christ. A compassionate servant feels deeply for the person who suffers but does not dwell there. Your compassion enables you to act. Now you are a co-laborer with Christ, clothed with compassion. Put it on, give it shape, practice it, pray for its release, and let it become your companion just as the Holy Spirit is your companion in ministry. Go fearlessly, when invited, into the darkness of a person's soul, knowing you walk in the light that darkness cannot ever overcome.

---

[1] Heidi Baker, *Compelled by Love* (Lake Mary, FL: Charisma House, 2008), 125-127.

A Prayer to Pray

Lord Jesus, teach me how to love the person in front of me. So often I fail to call to mind Your presence, ask for Your will, or give expression to Your desires for those I am with. If I look at myself, I just see my inadequacies, my fears, and my self-centeredness. When I look at You, I see pure love and fearlessness. I see the Father who sent His Son and the Son who left His place of equality with God to become a servant. Lord, keep my eyes upon You. As I look at You, I am free to love with Your love and to serve with Your heart. In You, I am courageous; in You, I have what it takes; in You I am empowered to fulfill Your purpose for today and the rest of my life.

I purpose to be Your instrument, a servant to those who are imprisoned by empty promises and in bondage to sin. I purpose to be a servant of Your compassion and truth. Lord, enlarge my heart; teach me how to love. Holy Spirit, show me the way of compassion.

Ministry…is simply about loving the person in front of you. It's about stopping for the one and being the very fragrance of Jesus to a lost and dying world.

Heidi Baker

PART II
Releasing the Gift of Freedom

The deep waters of a person's heart give the clearest picture of how evil spirits may be at work in him. For this reason, we place an emphasis in UNBOUND ministry on understanding the person rather than simply understanding the spiritual world and the work of spirits. If the enemy has access to the life of a believer, there is always a pathway he has used that needs to be discovered. That pathway can be shut down through faith in Christ. In this section, I want to help you understand how spirits work by focusing on understanding people and the very human pathway that the enemy takes to bring affliction and bondage. First, we will look at understanding people through guided listening. Second, we will learn to recognize the enemy's work. Third, we will follow it up with a discussion of how to look deeper—to the roots from which all the enemy's lies spring forth. Fourth, we will expose the working of self-justification. Finally, we will put this understanding to work as we pray for the Father's blessing to penetrate the human heart.

Chapter 5
Listening

When it's God speaking...the proper way to behave is to imitate someone who has an irresistible curiosity and who listens at keyholes. You must listen to everything God says at the keyhole of your heart. (ST. JOHN VIANNEY)

It is impossible to understand another person without listening to him. Even if you listen, your ability to understand is limited if you have not listened to your own heart and do not know your own soul. Listening is a challenge. We all need God's help to know the thoughts deep within us. If you or I go it alone, we could be in danger. Jeremiah 17:9 warns us that our hearts are full of deception: "The heart is deceitful above all things, and desperately corrupt; who can understand it?"

Left to ourselves, we may believe the darkness within that presents itself as light. If Satan can come disguised as an angel of light (2 Corinthians 11:14), it is clear that the deceptions buried within can present themselves as truth and righteousness. We may think control is responsible leadership and fear is prudence. Rather than recognizing how we are striving for acceptance, we will see only a desire for holiness; rather than arrogance, we will see self-confidence. Our hearts deceive us!

The apostle Paul, considering the sin that dwells within, says, "Wretched man that I am! Who will deliver me from this body of death? Thanks be to God through Jesus Christ our Lord!" (Romans 7:24-25). Jesus has delivered you. You are no longer subject to the power of sin and the unruly flesh; you have God's Spirit within you. This means you no longer listen simply to your heart but can now listen to God, who dwells in your heart by the Holy Spirit. You can understand God through the "keyhole" of your heart as you are being transformed and you can understand your own heart because you hear the truth of God.

The Spirit and the Word

Listening requires the guidance of the Spirit of God and the truth of His Word. His Word tells you Jesus has not left you an orphan; His Spirit dwells in you and is with you to lead you to truth:

> *And I will ask the Father, and he will give you another advocate to help you and be with you forever—the Spirit of truth. The world cannot accept Him, because it neither sees Him nor knows Him. But you know Him, for He lives with you and will be in you. I will not leave you as orphans; I will come to you.*
>
> John 14:16-18 (NIV)

You can rely on the promise of the continual presence of the Holy Spirit. The Spirit has been given to be your comforter, your counselor, your wisdom, and your guide. Jesus says, in John 16:13, "When the Spirit of truth comes, He will guide you into all the truth." First, the Spirit enables the church to faithfully preserve the revelation He entrusted to His body. He also is the "finger of God," guiding you to the truth of your own heart. You can trust Him to reveal areas of deception within or patterns of idolatry expressed in outward behaviors. As you read Scriptures, He will apply them to your heart.

For example, you may read in the Psalms, "How good and pleasant it is when brothers dwell in unity" (Psalm 133:1) and be convicted about your quarrel with a fellow church member. Or you may read in Proverbs that "anxiety in a man's heart weighs him down" (Proverbs 12:25) and realize for the first time that your struggle against depression may be rooted in fear. This is common when we ask the Spirit of God to reveal our hearts to us, for the Holy Spirit wields God's Word as a two-edged sword, making plain hidden thoughts and desires: "For the Word of God is living and active, sharper than any two-edged sword, piercing to the division of soul and spirit, of joints and marrow, and discerning the thoughts and intentions of the heart" (Hebrews 4:12).

Call on the Spirit and trust Him to guide you. If you call, of course you must learn to recognize His voice. In fact, God expects you to listen for His voice. Jesus said, "My sheep hear My voice, and I know them, and they follow Me" (John 10:27). At Jesus' baptism, the Father said from heaven, "This is my beloved Son, with whom I am well pleased; listen to Him" (Matthew 17:5). So how do you do that? The following five steps are a review of actions all believers can take to learn to listen to God. They should certainly operate in the life of those who are using the Five Keys of UNBOUND. Are you missing any of them?

1. Believe you can hear from God.

2. Ask Him to speak to you.

3. Make sure you ask with a desire to line up your thinking with His Word and become sensitive to His leading.

4. Ask that He make His will known—not only to you but also through you for the liberation of others. Remember that it is God's passion to set the captives free and He can use you no matter how you are feeling on a particular day. It is not about you!

5. Remember the decision you made to follow the Lord. Make daily decisions to surrender your will and sincerely seek Him for His will. Remember, it is the sheep that follow the shepherd that "hear His voice," and He has good things for all who call on His name.

Listening to God's whispers as the Lord uncovers the secrets of your heart is a solid foundation on which to begin to minister to others. It is extremely helpful for UNBOUND leaders to have received UNBOUND ministry and understand how to use the Five Keys in an ongoing way in their own lives. As you allow the Spirit and the Word of God to penetrate your heart, you are prepared to be an instrument for others.

An Open Heart

When someone comes for an UNBOUND ministry session, we hope they will come with an open heart. We want to help them hear God's voice. But what about the leader? Is your heart open? Your personal battle to yield your heart and will to God will give you compassion, along with wisdom and authority, for others. Struggling to hear God's voice in your own life, even while the Lord is using you to help others, will humble you. But that is good.

At times you may need a spiritual breakthrough in the atmosphere over your family, your ministry, or your church. The prophet Daniel needed a spiritual breakthrough for his people. He was in mourning, humbling himself before the Lord. After three weeks, the angel of the Lord appeared to Him.

> *Then he said to me, "Fear not, Daniel, for from the first day that you set your mind to understand and humbled yourself before your God, your words have been heard, and I have come because of your words. The prince of the kingdom of Persia withstood me twenty-one days; but Michael, one of the chief princes, came to help me, so I left him there with the prince of the kingdom of Persia."*
>
> Daniel 10:12-13

God had heard his prayer on the first day, but there was a battle to be fought. Daniel needed to persevere in prayer and fasting until the messenger brought God's Word to him. If you too need a breakthrough in the spiritual atmosphere, God is faithful and He will give a breakthrough to those who ask. He wants you to continue to knock on the door like the man who asked his neighbor for bread and like the persistent widow who sought redress from the judge. Heart of the Father Ministries and the message of UNBOUND were birthed out of my encounters with the Lord that followed times of prayer, fasting, testing, and more prayer. As God gave me grace to persevere in prayer before the Lord, He gave me more territory. He will give you new levels of responsibility too as you fight to gain and then guard the territory He has promised you.

At other times, you may need a personal breakthrough. Satan wants to bring you under condemnation for your sins. If you become aware of stubbornness or willfulness, you may think "How can I ever hear from God, since I am such a mess? How could He use me?" Or you may negatively compare yourself to others who heard the Lord tell them to do something; when they obeyed, miracles followed. Comparing yourself to others will only foster discouragement, and looking inward at yourself never helps you hear God's voice. If you bring your awareness of your sin and weakness to God, He will keep you from unbelief and doubt.

What happens if you have allowed bitterness to return to your heart? Perhaps you sought God a long time, asking Him to speak about some practical things like decisions you needed to make, your finances, your future, or whatever you have been tempted to worry about, but you have not heard an answer. You may no longer seek God's voice because you are disappointed, confused, or disillusioned. Your heart may have become hard. The writer to the Hebrews warns against hardness of heart when he says, "So, as the Holy Spirit says, 'Today, if you hear His voice, do not harden your hearts as you did in the rebellion'… See to it, brothers that none of you has a sinful, unbelieving heart that turns away from the living God" (Hebrews 3:7-8a, 12 NIV).

In that chapter, the writer of Hebrews gives the antidote to hardness of heart: fix your eyes on Jesus and seek encouragement from your fellow believers. I will also add: seek to live in the truth. The thought that God does not care (or is not strong enough or is silent) is always a lie. God is not silent. If you have not received the answers you want, the truth is that the circumstances which concern you the most are secondary to His greater purpose for your life. The Holy Spirit will use every opportunity to expose the deception in your heart. He is revealing what is within so he can lead you out of areas of captivity.

Are you yourself bound? The way to overcome your own sinful patterns and gain an open heart to God is to repent and believe. Humbly repent of sin, of willfulness, of pride, of comparison, of unbelief, and of a hard heart. Turn to God and believe that no matter how rebellious or stubborn you may have been, God is bigger than all sin and He is able to lead anyone, including you, to freedom. If you turn to Him and seek to hear His voice, He will speak. He is bigger than all your faults. After you have repented, take time in personal prayer to ask to hear His voice and then set yourself to listen through reading His Word. Allow your imagination to be captured by His presence. Seek God throughout the day and expect God to speak through circumstances and people. As you minister to others, build on these foundation stones. The more you learn to listen to God and the more you go through the battle of overcoming any hardness of heart and any deceptions you still carry, the better prepared you will be to be used by God to help others open their hearts to Him as well.

God's Helper

An open heart in the one who comes for prayer ministry is a gift of God's grace working in cooperation with His own will. But you can assist by offering prayer, presence, purpose, and protection.

- ✥ Prayer for the person coming for ministry is a vital first step. Pray for them before they even walk in the door. Open the session with prayer for them. Jesus says He stands at the door and knocks; He wants to come in. Your prayers will help the person open their heart.

- ✥ The presence of God is important in a ministry session, so invoke God's presence as you begin and remain aware of God's presence throughout the session. His presence will release His compassion. His compassion will open the heart.

- ✥ Listen with purpose. Many people have told their stories repeatedly, sometimes to counselors who left them disappointed after weeks or months of sharing. They may have lost hope. They may be tired and wonder if God is listening. Your purpose in listening is to lead them to respond to the Lord using the Five Keys. If they understand your purpose, there is a greater possibility for renewed hope. This hope often comes when they read UNBOUND or attend a conference. It can also come in other ways as local ministries proclaim the gospel or teach the Five Keys. Hope opens the heart.

- ✥ Offer Protection. Hearts are open when a person feels protected. If they know the ministry room is a safe place and their secrets will be kept confidential, they will be released from fears that keep their heart closed. It is common to hear a person say at the end of a session they never told anyone this before in their life.

When prayer, presence, purpose, and protection work together, the Holy Spirit moves in amazing ways. Often, a person will spend the first ten minutes of a session talking about the most superficial things. I listen and pray and sometimes wonder why they came for UNBOUND ministry. Once they consciously (or even unconsciously) have tested me and realized they are safe, they are going to be listened to and accepted rather than judged, they are able to move to the most critical issues for their deliverance. You will experience the same pattern.

Practical Ways to Listen

Every time you listen to a story and help someone take hold of their freedom, you are learning about people and their response to the traumas of life; you are learning how evil spirits interact with the darkness within and you are learning how to love. This is on-the-job training that prepares you to serve someone in the future whom you have not yet met. As you listen, quickly write down areas that may need repentance, people who need to be forgiven, and spirits and lies that need to be renounced. Many of the things that need to be renounced are obvious right from the start of the interview: occult practice, fear of rejection, fornication, hatred, revenge, and so on. It is possible you will hear words that will lead you to ask about other things: "You mentioned loneliness; do you struggle with feeling isolated?" Loneliness and isolation are often connected. Sometimes the person needs help to express aspects of loneliness or the consequences of loneliness that have not been named.

In the back of this guidebook, we have provided a sheet called "Learning to Listen."[1] You may wish to use this as a guide to listen according to the Five Keys of UNBOUND. The form gives space to jot down significant points in the story. Remember—you will want to listen for tactics of the enemy because you want to help the one who came for prayer take their own stand against the those tactics. Listening requires trust in the Holy Spirit. Believe that as you have an interview (conversation) with the Five Keys in mind, the Holy Spirit will reveal what is hidden. As you listen, take care to focus on the one who came for ministry rather than on your notes. Listen to the story with deep interest, compassion, and love, jotting down clues that will lead to

---

[1] See Appendix B, p. 206

deeper insight, but do not interrupt the flow. There will be time to ask questions and fill in the blanks of the story later.

If the seeker feels safe and understood, they will open the doors to what God is doing in their heart to set them free. Your continued prayer can be, "Lord, send the Holy Spirit to help them share what is most important today and help me to listen and hear what the Father is doing." As you write down key words that the person mentions (e.g., *loneliness, hopelessness, timidity*...), expect to gain some understanding of patterns of behavior, patterns of reaction, and patterns of interaction. Look for ways these patterns interrelate. How have lies become manifest and how have they become intertwined in the person's way of thinking and personality? What are the significant entryways for the enemy? What is the person's most basic response to life? When they were young, did they respond to chaos in the home by withdrawing or attacking? Is this pattern true today? Are their root motivations fear or self-protection?

Jesus said, "For there is nothing hid, except to be made manifest; nor is anything secret, except to come to light. If any man has ears to hear, let him hear" (Mark 4:22-23).

If you have ears to hear, you will see these patterns reveal a person's basic response to life. If they have undergone pastoral counseling or received spiritual direction and have insight already, they may just lay it out there for you, in which case you may simply confirm it and help them process it. Sometimes the patterns only begin to be clear as they share about past relationships and the traumas of life. At some point, ask about their relationship with their parents when they were young.[2] Patterns develop early and repeat in the circumstances of life. They repeat until they are redeemed. So many people think a sinful pattern is just "my personality" or just "the way our family is." You can help them identify and name the faulty foundation stones they have built their lives upon. You can help them see they can be freed from generational patterns as well as from their own sinful responses to life. By doing

---

[2] It is normally best to save this question until after you have had an opportunity to observe what is being expressed both in current events and in the historical situation.

this, you will move from simply trying to help the person name their enemies or group of enemies to understanding people.

Wow! That's a lot. Beginners in UNBOUND ministry should not dwell on the last paragraph. Do not be intimidated. God teaches these things one person at a time. The important thing to know is He is always teaching and you are always learning. Come back to this paragraph and review it after ministering. Amazingly, God will have taught you what you need to know. The five keys are simple yet profound. By God's grace, you will understand everything you need to help a person in bondage, but there will always be more to learn about understanding people.

Once the interview ends, go over with the person what you have written down. You may not yet understand how it all fits together, but if you can give the person some understanding of how one thing leads to another, they will gain insights that will help protect them from deception and help them maintain and grow in their freedom. I will often get further understanding as I explain back what I heard in their story and how I would like to lead them through the first three keys. Other times, this insight comes to me as I listen to them repent, forgive, and renounce. **If I can point out patterns of response that have repeated in their lives, they will begin to see how they have made a home for lies; they will better understand their enemies and be aware of their areas of weakness and bondage.**

In listening, be guided by the principles you have learned, by experience in your past, and by the grace of the Holy Spirit. Guided listening is exciting. Through guided listening, you will get to see the Lord uncover what is hidden in the heart. If you understand people and if you understand how lies have opened the door to the enemy, you can experience the great honor of having fellowship with the Spirit as Jesus sets the captive free to the glory of God the Father. The objective for all of those who serve is to move beyond self-reliance or reliance on some "method" to greater reliance on the work of the Holy Spirit. Always remember this is the Lord's work; He is using you and He is able to use a humble servant even if you feel totally lost. You will gain the deepest insights as you battle to trust the Lord and as you listen to and love the person He has sent to you. Through your listening and praying, you help usher in the kingdom of God.

We anticipate the day when all know the Lord in freedom. "And no longer shall each man teach his neighbor and each his brother, saying, 'Know the Lord,' for they shall all know Me, from the least of them to the greatest, says the Lord; for I will forgive their iniquity, and I will remember their sin no more" (Jeremiah 31:34).

The Holy Spirit enables all believers to know the Lord personally. He empowers you to see Him and to hear His voice. Give that gift to another by listening well.

❖   ❖   ❖

CHAPTER 6

Recognizing the Enemy

Don't you believe that there is in man a deep so profound as to be hidden even to him in whom it is? (SAINT AUGUSTINE)

Young children have no control over what happens to them or the circumstances of their lives. All they can do is respond to life around them, whether it is chaotic and dysfunctional or stable and loving. The choices children make as they interpret their experiences are influenced more by personality and their parents than by reason. Every child, therefore, responds and interprets in ways that are particular to him. Two children, in one family, with similar experiences, may react to the same circumstance in very different ways.

As a child grows, these responses become patterns of behavior and thinking. Many of the patterns are negative, but if the child or young adult seeks to follow God, they will struggle to overcome the negative patterns through repentance and the effort to renew their mind. Unfortunately, sometimes a pattern becomes so familiar that the individual does not realize there is a problem. He or she may excuse it as no big deal or perhaps identify with it and say, "This is just the way I am" or "All the men (or women) in our family are arrogant." Negative patterns may be so much a part of them that the thought of living without them triggers insecurity. They may think, "If I let that go, then who will I be?" Patterns of thinking and behavior that are a response to early experiences become part of their identity and survival strategy. If you can understand typical patterns that develop from responses to past interactions with the outside world, you will be better able to understand people and to understand the ways in which evil spirits afflict them.

Exorcists look for demons. Some healing ministries look for wounds an individual has suffered so they can invite the love of God into the memory for healing. In UNBOUND ministry, we are more interested in helping each person identify and understand how they have responded (and continue to respond) to the world around them and to the wounds of life. What are the patterns of thought that have become deeply entrenched? These patterns are often provoked and rear their ugly heads by some current circumstance that reminds the individual of a dark memory from the past. Until the initial trauma and their subsequent response is brought into the open by the work of the Holy Spirit, the power of these negative emotional and psychological responses will manage to compromise their faith in Jesus, their baptism, and their life as a disciple of the Lord. Fortunately, the Holy Spirit knows the heart and loves to bring revelation in a multitude of ways.

The UNBOUND interview exposes sin, reveals the work of the flesh, brings to light the effects of the world, and uncovers the schemes of the devil by first uncovering what is hidden in the human heart. Evil spirits have the ability to hold a person in bondage if they are in agreement with the spirits in some significant way. If you can help them understand the enemy's influence has come through seduction, not invasion, they will know how to take their stand.[1] Since this agreement comes because of deception and sin, their deliverance will come as they believe in the mercy of God and exchange the lie for the truth. The truth of God closes the entry point, or door of access, to their heart. When this is done, spirits must go.

---

[1] The case could be made that with children, demons invade innocence. Seduction requires cooperation with the deceiver. In the case of a child, the parents are seduced to be the doorway. As the child grows into an adult, there is a point where they either reject the lie or accept it, affirming their agreement with the spirits that have a hold on them. Each person has made this choice, and now they must be helped to take responsibility, no matter how limited that choice was or what evil was brought upon them when they were young.

Spirits and Lies

A lie is anything that is contrary to the revelation of God in Jesus Christ. Any thought, philosophy, or logic that veils the reality of God's love and distorts human dignity is a lie. Jesus told us Satan is the father of lies. If you wish to understand people and the effect of spirits in their lives, learn to recognize the lies that have been believed. As I wrote on page 108 of *Resisting the Devil*:

> Spirits are present wherever they focus their attention. When we sin, they are drawn like flies. If they perceive our vulnerability to sin, they will focus on it. If we sin and do not repent quickly, they will present to us thoughts and images that justify our sin, or draw us into deeper agreement with our sin. The lies that are a part of every sin find a place to be rooted within our hearts. As our thoughts agree with the enemies' lies, they become entangled not just with a false thought, but with the spirit behind it.

And again on page 157:

> Like flies attracted to fresh manure, evil spirits appear instantaneously in the presence of sin. As they perceive rebellion of any sort, they come to bring greater destructive influence. They will bring thoughts of self-justification, blame, excuses, bitterness, false judgments, destructive criticism, self-condemnation, or self-rejection to build a fortress around the foothold they have already gained.

As you look for the possible expression of the work of evil spirits in the one who came for prayer, help them renounce spirits and lies, thereby closing the pathway of entry.

Grouping of Spirits

In 1973, Frank and Ida Mae Hammond published *Pigs in the Parlor*. In this book, the Hammonds placed a list of common demonic groupings of spirits that they had uncovered during their years of work in deliverance ministry. Many people simply took the list and cast out all the spirits. This was not the authors' intention. They wrote the following in capital letters: "THESE GROUPINGS ARE ONLY SUGGESTIVE OF WHAT MAY BE ENCOUNTERED. THE LISTING IS BY NO MEANS INTENDED

TO BE EXHAUSTIVE OR THE GROUPS TO BE INVARIABLE."[2] They also wrote that the possibilities for grouping are unlimited. The list was not to be a substitute for listening to the Holy Spirit or to the person who came for prayer.

Knowing very little about deliverance as a young Christian, I did not understand the connection between groupings of spirits and the person's life and personality. I had an overly spiritual view that sought to discern these spirits and cast them out. Through the years, I have found this list helpful, but in the beginning I did not understand that these spirits and the groupings mirrored things in the person's life that needed the application of the first three keys—repentance and faith, forgiveness, and renunciation.

Because of the way I had seen this list used, I held back from using a list in our training for many years. Now I know how beneficial such a list can be—it can help you learn how to assist others. If you understand groupings of spirits and become familiar with a list of groupings, you can more effectively help a person name what is at work inside them and lead them to deeper insight. If this information is used correctly, it will help the one who comes for prayer identify their enemies and understand the spiritual bondage they experience—bondage that comes through their very human responses to life. If used properly, a list of groupings can be a starting point to help you, the interviewer, understand the person you are listening to. It can help you communicate so that someone understands.

I have developed my own list, found in Appendix B.[3] It looks a bit like the Hammonds' list but is shorter. It is shorter because I did not run into the same things they did. Traveling to different countries and working in different cultures helps me understand we must not

---

[2] Frank and Ida Mae Hammond, *Pigs in the Parlor* (Kirkwood, MO: Impact Christian Books, 1973), 113.

[3] See pp. 211-212 of Appendix B. The objective for all who serve is to move beyond reliance on the list to greater reliance on the work of the Holy Spirit. Always remember that this is the Lord's work. He is using you and He is able to use a humble servant even if you feel totally lost at times. The deepest insights are usually gained as you battle to trust the Lord, listening and loving the person He has sent to you.

be limited to a list. Though you may feel more comfortable with a list if you are just beginning to minister using the UNBOUND model, it is more important for you to have a way of listening that helps each person identify the entryway and the lie that opened the door to the enemy. For example, in one country Janet and I prayed for a number of people who had come under the influence of a woman who used eggs to give spiritual direction. We never found a word to give a description of what was going on, so we just had her renounce the spirit at work in the person who did something with eggs. This worked fine. You will not find this on any list!

COMMON SENSE AND WISDOM

The Lord offers you both common sense and supernatural wisdom to understand people. He expects you to use both gifts to love the one who sits in front of you. You know that minor bondage can lead to deeper entrapment, and bondage in one area may lead to bondage in another. For example, when the Scriptures warn against letting the sun go down on anger, it means anger can provide an opening for the enemy. Anger is a God-given emotion. It is intended to motivate a person to action, to lead them to resolve, to change, and to make decisions: "Tomorrow morning, I am going to tell my co-worker how offensive his language is to me. Forgive me, Lord, for my thoughts of retaliation and for thinking such negative judgments about him. Help me to speak the truth in love. Amen." If this person does not resolve to forgive and to deal with the offense but instead nurtures their anger, the anger will grow. They have now added unforgiveness, resentment, and bitterness. Soon they may begin to have thoughts of hatred for their co-worker and think of retaliation or revenge. Hatred can lead to violence. If they live with hatred long enough (or give in to violence), they may take pleasure in thinking of their co-worker's death or even fantasize about killing him. They are now in bondage to a spirit of violence and a spirit of murder.

As you interview, listen for any one of those words. Now, you will have a basis to delve deeper:

"You mentioned anger a number of times; do you struggle with resentment?"

"Yes."
"How about bitterness?"
"Yes."
"Has it ever grown to hatred?"
"Yes."
"Did you ever wish they were dead or entertain thoughts about murder?"

A person may be aware of the anger and rage they are bound by but have never recognized the deeper bondage that came along with it. Unresolved anger and unforgiveness, you see, can lead to bitterness, revenge (or retaliation), hatred, rage, violence, and even murder. If people are brought to the Lord, though, they can now name their enemies and renounce them in the name that is above all names.

That is just one example of how spirits are related. Another common grouping is those spirits that cluster around pride. Rebellion and disobedience, as well as self-justification, self-righteousness, perfectionism, striving, and stubbornness are some examples. Pride is also the root of self-hatred, self-rejection, and self-criticism—and it may lead to bondage to a critical spirit and judgments that could then lead to isolation and loneliness. Pride is a block to forgiving oneself. Ultimately, pride is simply a cover up for insecurity. Learn from the list provided in the appendix, but again, depend on the Holy Spirit to guide you to see patterns and connections as you listen in love.

When listening to a person's story, listen also for lies that they have believed. Lies are as unique as each person is and as varied as all the people who ever lived. Though I have included a list of lies in the appendix, do not assume the list is exhaustive. There are some common threads to lies, however: lies that tear down a person's identity, lies that deny the truth about who God is, and lies that destroy hope for the future. For example, you may hear a person say "It's always my fault," "God doesn't want to help me," or even "I will never get out from under this." Evil spirits hide beneath the lies we have swallowed in the same way that crabs hide under rocks near the jetty on Long Island's Jones Beach.

As you lead the person to renounce the lie, the spirit's power is broken. On numerous occasions, I have seen people set free as they renounced the lie that "something is wrong with me." This lie is an expression of shame; behind it is very likely a spirit of shame. Where does such a lie come from? Well, something traumatic may have happened to the person when they were young; perhaps the parents divorced, leading them to experience rejection and abandonment. They then interpreted the experience, and in their young mind, the conviction grew: "It is my fault. Something is wrong with me." For some people, this lie is close to the surface–they know they think this and have even expressed these words. They actively believe the lie. For others, the lie is more hidden. If it pops up, they push it down, either because they know intellectually it's not the truth or because the thought is too threatening and provokes fear. "What if it is true? What will I do then? It is better to just avoid it." These fearful thoughts reveal they may be overwhelmed and feeling hopeless.

Several months after attending an UNBOUND conference, Susan knew she was not free. She had had a very difficult relationship with her now deceased father. She always told herself that even though the relationship was painful, her father loved her. In fact, that morning—in speaking with her mother—she said those very words: "At least I know Dad loved me." A few hours later, while taking a shower, her eyes were opened. She saw the lie she had really believed hidden under her words: "My dad did not love me!" She knew what to do. She found her husband and said, "I know what I need to renounce." Susan renounced the lie and took authority over it in the name of Jesus. At that point, she was set free and her life was changed.

A Captive Set Free

In Charlotte's story below, you will see how deeply bondage grows out of foundational lies.

> When I was seven, I saw my mother kissing another man, and I told my dad. Their already rocky marriage ended, and my dad became a Saturday dad. I was devastated, I was so hurt, and I blamed myself for having told. I was convinced it was my fault my father went away. That was the lie that I believed vehemently, and I hated myself because of it. I lashed out at God. I said I hated Him too, and in my pain, I would not forgive myself or God.

For almost forty years, I struggled with the effects of that lie in my life. Blaming and punishing myself became a habit that eventually became a compulsion. Soon more and more things became "my fault." If someone was unhappy or upset, it was my fault. If someone got angry, somehow it was my fault. The lies just kept multiplying, and eventually I became a compulsive pleaser.

As I grew both in age and in character, I began to walk with the Lord again, but my habit of punishing and blaming myself was a part of everything I did, and got in the way of every relationship I had. People liked me because most of the time I did what they wanted, but inside I hated myself. I couldn't forgive myself. And because I couldn't forgive, I couldn't believe that God was forgiving and merciful. God's mercy was for everyone but me.

About a year ago, my spiritual director gave me a copy of UNBOUND: *A Practical Guide to Deliverance*. After reading it, I wanted to run to Pennsylvania. But I waited until they had a conference. At first, I called Heart of the Father Ministries and spoke with Jenn. After hearing my story, she said, "This is not God's plan for your life!" No one had said that to me before. The lies were buried so deep that I thought they were me. I thought this was just the way I was; that this is the way life is.

At the conference, Jenn prayed with me. At first, I couldn't even say the words "I renounce the lie that it's my fault that my dad went away." After almost forty years of unforgiveness and blame, I was stuck and it was demonic. But she just quietly kept praying with me. I have this image that the lie was a big weed the size of a sapling and her prayers were the shovel digging around the base of this weed until it just popped out, and I was finally able to say, from my heart, "It's not my fault." The weight of forty years was lifted off me. I was delivered. I was truly set free in a way I never thought possible. This was the beginning of an ongoing process of transformation that continues today."

Charlotte may have had a predisposition toward believing "it's all my fault" that predated her mother's kiss with another man. But the resultant separation of her parents brought the predisposition to life and gave the lie such intense power. She tried to run from the lie by controlling her relationships, trying to keep them from falling apart, but it did no good.

Remember that lies may be dealt with by naming and renouncing the lie or by renouncing the spirit. For example, you may have an individual renounce the lie "I am a failure" or renounce a spirit of failure. You may suggest they renounce the lie "I am not a good father (or mother)" or encourage them to renounce self-rejection, self-criticism, and self-accusation. The lie "no one needs me" may be dealt with as they renounce self-pity. It does not matter whether the person names the spirits behind the statements or simply renounces the lies. When you break the power and command the spirit to leave in the name of Jesus, the power of the false thinking will be broken as well. If there is something hidden that God still wants to deal with at that time, you can trust it will surface after the command.

Curses, Vows, and Judgments

A curse is a source of spiritual harm. It can come in many ways: from someone invoking an evil spirit to bring evil, to words pronounced by a fortuneteller or psychic declaring something about the individual's future, to negative words that either they or significant people in their life spoke over them, to occult spells and objects in their possession.

During the interview, you want to uncover any access point the enemy has found. Your mission is to help people who believe they are under a curse know the truth of who they are in Christ and the limits of the devil's power. You will help them deal with fear. One way to do this is to help them see why they were vulnerable to a curse or open to believing the lie that a curse is the source of their spiritual problems. Proverbs 26:2 reads, "Like a fluttering sparrow or a darting swallow, an undeserved curse does not come to rest" (NIV). For a curse to find a place in believers, it has to have a place to rest. An individual must have received it for it to be effective. What are common access doors for a curse to take root? Primary ones are fear, unbelief, and a lack of boundaries.

Breaking a curse is not a very difficult thing to do. You know from Unbound teaching to have the person renounce "the spirit that came when…" You break the power of every negative word and then you command the spirit that entered to leave. If the curse was put on them by another, have them say, "I renounce the spirit that was at work in _____ and I break the power of the words or ritual that was done." If they voluntarily opened themselves up to a spirit, lead them to repent and renounce it by saying, "I renounce the spirit that operated in _____ (identify the person) and I take back the authority I gave to the person." Once this is done, you, as the leader, should command the spirit to leave in Jesus' name.

It is unlikely a person's affliction is solely from a curse. Before you command the spirit to leave, you should investigate the interrelationship of lies and spirits in the person's life. Get the bigger picture of other entryways. Find out why they were subject to a curse. Was it unbelief, fear, or superstition? What effect did thinking they were cursed have on them? Did it lead to fear, anxiety, or religiosity? A curse becomes powerful and more difficult to break in a person's life when it finds its ways into their personality and entwines itself among the web of hurts, insecurities, and fears.

Vows

When painful events overtake a person's life, they may be tempted to avoid that part of life that has caused them so much pain. If they were deserted by someone they loved, they may be tempted to say, "I'm never going to love again" or "I will never trust a man (or woman) again." These are vows that act like strong iron bars around their life. To break a vow, simply have them repeat, "In the name of Jesus, I renounce the vow I made when I said ___ and I break its power over me." Actually renouncing the vow may be more helpful than just renouncing mistrust, rejection, hurt, unforgiveness, or "the lie that I cannot trust a man (or woman)." Actually renouncing the vow with specific words breaks its power because the doorway to the bondage was the pronouncement, the utterance of the spoken word.

Negative judgments may act like curses and can remain for a lifetime. These too are lies to be renounced, but acknowledging negative words and forgiving the one who spoke them is the foundation for breaking their power. Negative judgments from others include statements like, "You weren't an accident; you were a mistake," "You will never amount to anything," or "If you're fat, no one will marry (love) you." Lead the one who came for prayer to forgive the one who spoke those words and renounce the lie that came to them in the form of judgment. Sometimes negative judgments come from within. If the one to whom you minister says things like "I am ugly," "I will never be good enough," or "I fail at everything," have them repent and then renounce the lie they spoke.

It is possible a person is actually in bondage because of judgments they have made toward others. If this is the case, move back to the first key and lead them in repentance. They may think they are "protecting" themselves from harm when they make unrighteous judgments against family members or significant people God placed in their life, but they have actually cut themselves off from the love they have to give them. If they judge others as a self-protective mechanism, they lock themselves up in a prison, restricting their own emotional development. What they have judged in others will limit their ability to see the truth in themselves and to grow, which will often lead them to become like the person they have judged.[4] If they say, "I will never be like my mother/father," or "My father/mother is worthless," they must repent for their judgments ("Lord, forgive me for judging my mom and withholding my heart from her"). Like it or not, they are like their parents. They need to separate from their sin and from generational sin, but if they reject their parents, they are also rejecting a part of themselves that needs to be accepted so it can come to maturity.

FREELY GIVE

It took many years for me to move away from a super spiritual understanding of spirits as mysterious entities that would invade human beings and that were separate from their human experience. But I have learned to listen for the very human responses people make in life and to the words they use to describe what goes on within. Using common sense, and being guided by the Holy Spirit, I can help people take their

---

[4] See *The Older Brother Returns* (Clinton Corners, NY: Attic Studio Press, 1995), 85-102.

stand against the enemy's schemes by using the Five Keys. I have given this understanding away through my books and conferences, and you have received it. Now you too can listen to men and women and help them repent, forgive, and renounce the lies (the spirits that empower the lies) that have found a way into their hearts. By God's grace, you can lead the ones who come to you for prayer into the heart of the Father to receive His blessing. This is the ministry Jesus has entrusted to you.

CHAPTER 7
Understanding Foundational Patterns

In what does the human being's wretchedness actually consist? Above all, in his insecurity; in the uncertainties with which he is burdened; in the limitations that oppress him; in the lack of freedom that binds him; in the pain that makes his life hateful to him. Ultimately there is, behind all this, the meaninglessness of his existence.

We can say, then, that the root of man's wretchedness is loneliness, is the absence of love—is the fact that my existence is not embraced by a love that makes it necessary...what man needs is a communion that goes beyond [everything and] reaches deep into the heart of man and endures even in death.

Pope Benedict XVI[1]

As you pray for people, you will begin to notice certain patterns in the responses people have toward the events in their lives. Each person has their own patterns of response, but all of us embrace similar patterns as we react to the destructive power of sin at work in the human nature we share. As we recognize these foundational patterns in our lives, expose them by their roots, and embrace the truth that sets us free, we can, by the grace of God, help others break from the grip of these patterns.

---

[1] *Principles of Catholic Theology: Building Stones for a Fundamental Theology* (San Fransisco: Ignatius, 1987), 52.

Lucifer's Strategy

Our basic patterns of response to life can be traced back through the original sin of Adam and Eve to Lucifer, the initiator of all sin. No sin existed before Lucifer sinned. Sin belonged to him and the third of the angels standing with him who were cast out of heaven. Their proud rejection of God became their identity and now their presence is the power behind our sin. We can understand the nature of Lucifer's sin by what he offered to Adam and Eve: he tempted them to seek to be God's equal, to reject God as God through an act of disobedience, and to choose their own way over their relationship with God. Lucifer's approach was subtle; because he could not enter and corrupt the human heart without human permission, he needed to seduce them.

The first step in Satan's plan of attack was to create doubt about God's Word. He had but to ask, "Did God *really* say…?" And Eve began to wonder. His second step was to challenge God's Word. He flatly contradicted it. "You will surely not die," he said to Eve. And this challenge brought Eve to step three: suspicion of God's motives and character. She listened when Satan said, "God knows…your eyes will be opened and you will be like God, knowing good and evil." Eve wondered, she doubted, she listened to the lie. Satan did not present the hook in a vacuum. No, it was cleverly disguised behind the goodness of the fruit. Eve saw the desirability of the fruit and the wisdom it could bring. *Beautiful…and oh so delicious…I will be wise…* She came under deception and that deception obscured the clear command of the Lord. She deliberately ate the fruit; she "also gave some to her husband." This was their step of pride and rebellion. Immediately, fear and insecurity sprang to life.

No one will ever be able to adequately explain what led Eve and then Adam to choose self-sufficiency over love. However, I would like to offer a possible explanation as to why this choice was a real temptation. There is vulnerability inherent in every true relationship. You are vulnerable, I am vulnerable, and Adam and Eve were vulnerable—for in a relationship of love, there is always vulnerability and therefore risk. M. Scott Peck writes, "There can be no vulnerability without risk; there can be no community without vulnerability; there can be no peace, and ultimately no life, without community."[2] It is good to be vulnerable, for vulnerability is an expression of freedom. In our vulnerability, we must trust: we must trust another to know us completely and still accept us. We must trust another's acceptance of our gift of ourselves. Trust is the gift of God, for it is in trusting that we fully know God. In trusting, we are fully known by Him.

As long as Adam and Eve were covered by the presence of God, they were secure, even though vulnerable. Once they rejected God and stepped outside of His presence by believing Satan's lie and disobeying the Lord's command, they were separated from God's love. Now they experienced fear, for insecurity had become a part of the human condition. No longer just a temptation, insecurity was alive in them as they hid from the One they once walked with in the cool of the evening. So it is with us. Now we too struggle to believe, to trust, and to obey. No matter how hard we try, we cannot overcome this insecurity by our own efforts. We are left with two choices: either we respond to insecurity by living in fear or we try to hide our insecurity with pride. These two responses are the twin roots of our foundational pattern and must be understood in relationship to each other and to the insecurity that lies beneath them. For sin is not only an act but also a power working within the human heart. "For I do not do the good I want, but the evil I do not want is what I do. Now if I do what I do not want, it is no longer I that do it, but sin which dwells within me" (Romans 7:19-20). If you can comprehend how the power of sin works in all of us through fear and pride, you will have a better understanding of yourself and those you seek to help.

The Sinful Nature as a Tree

To understand how the power of sin works in our lives, let us imagine the sinful human nature as a tree (see Figure A) planted next to a swamp. Like all trees, this tree draws its strength, stability, and sustenance from its root system. The trunk, branches, and leaves are

---

[2] M. Scott Peck, *The Different Drum: Community Making and Peace* (New York: Simon and Schuster, 1998), 233.

all expressions of what is going on below the surface. Therefore, let us examine this tree from its source to its branches. The swamp represents the power of sin, which characterizes Lucifer in his pride-filled rebellion against God. The swamp itself provides no solid soil for stability, so the state of this tree is unstable, which is characteristic of the insecurity that is part of the human condition apart from God. In an effort to support itself, the tree sends its roots to draw deeply on the decay and death in the swamp, bringing disorder to the trunk and branches.

The twin root system is fear and pride. Both are human responses to the insecurity that results from separation from God, and both represent how the power of sin works in a person's life. Therefore, they are inseparable and present in the sinful nature of everyone to whom we minister. Fear and pride come as a package deal, like two sides of a coin. One side is visible on the surface; the other is also present but hidden underneath. Sometimes it will appear as though pride is most active in a person's life, expressed in arrogance, rebellion, willfulness, or other ways. But beneath the pride is the root of fear in response to insecurity. Likewise, it may appear as though fear is most evident in a person's life, expressed in insecurity, anxiety, or even humility (a false humility). But beneath the fear is the root of pride. On rare occasions, we see an interesting and equal mixture of fear and pride. Because most people will identify with one of the two roots, they often do not see the other root lurking unexposed and therefore unaddressed. They also fail to see the insecurity that drives them both.

Two people, even two siblings, will have very different responses to abandonment or rejection based upon their God-given personalities, the uniqueness of their experience, and the way they chose to interpret the rejection and abandonment they suffered. The first responded to life from childhood with aggression and rebellion. They became someone who is quick to attack and to blame. Their anger is out of control. For them, pride will be most evident. The second person responded in childhood by withdrawing and blaming themselves for the rejection. For them, insecurity is more easily recognized. As a broken person looking for love, they do not readily identify with pride. They have simply been trying to survive the chaos. They are overwhelmed by the idea that they have pride. Alternatively, the arrogant one revels in

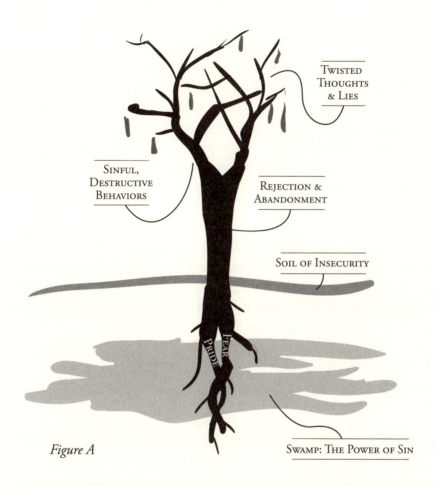

Figure A

their "me first" way of living, dismissing the idea that they have deep insecurities and fear.

How can you examine the roots? By examining the branches. The branches of a tree reflect what is going on in the roots below the surface. The branches will reveal what the roots are drawing into the trunk, whether the roots drink health or disease. The branches of our swamp-bound tree correspond to the spirits and lies that are referred to in the last chapter. These spirits and lies are expressions of fear and pride. As you interview people, you will discover their expressions of each. Pride may show itself in rebellion, disobedience, willfulness, self-sufficiency, independence, self-reliance, self-justification, self-righteousness, perfectionism, stubbornness, argumentativeness, superiority, and arrogance. Fear may show itself in self-justification, perfectionism, control, argumentativeness, and stubbornness. Why are the expressions so much the same? Because fear will turn to pride for safety.

It is rare for a person to have all of these expressions of fear and pride to a level that they all need to be renounced. Usually a person has a set or two connected expressions from the above lists. For example, self-justification, self-righteousness, perfectionism, and stubbornness are commonly found together. Another set might be self-sufficiency, independence, and self-reliance. If some of these expressions come up in the interview, you can later ask about the others. You might ask, "Did you ever go through a time in your life of significant rebellion? Do you know what self-justification is? Can you see how that is connected to pride?" Or if the individual experiences a fear of everything falling apart, you might gently explain that fear often brings along with it issues with control. You might ask, "How do you react when things don't go your way? When you are wrong do you admit it readily or make excuses, wanting to blame someone else?" If they know they are not being judged, they will find that uncovering and naming enemies like self-righteousness or control, combined with renunciation, will be very empowering.

Do you understand the pattern? Pride and fear are tangled roots. Pride, with expressions such as judgment, criticism, comparison, or self-protection, is the effort to overcome fear, the root that is less visible, and the underlying insecurity that drives it. Fears and insecurities support pride and result from pride. As you listen to someone tell their story, listen for key words they use so you can help them understand their patterns. Do they call themselves a *perfectionist*? Do they talk about trying *real hard* to do everything right? If they deny resenting their parents for holding too high a standard but admit to *hating themselves*, you may want to ask if they have trouble *forgiving themselves*.

One reason people find it so hard to forgive themselves is that pride demands they be good enough to earn God's love. You may now recognize patterns that reveal pride or fear, but it is always a good idea to ask the individual if they themselves can see connections. You may say something like, "Do words like *shame, guilt,* or *self-condemnation* connect to your sense of worthlessness? How about *self-rejection, self-accusation*? They are often connected to the self-hatred you mentioned. Do you know what self-righteousness is? Self-justification? Could that be at the bottom of your perfectionism? Do you know the difference between seeking excellence for the glory of God and perfectionism rooted in fear?"

Always, as you listen, ask the Lord for understanding: "Lord, what can I ask that will help them understand their heart and put a name on the enemies they have made a home for?"

Now that you understand the twin roots of pride and fear, you may be tempted to presume you must deal with those immediately or you may be tempted to stop and teach each person about pride and insecurity. This would be inappropriate. Follow the lead of the Holy Spirit. Wait until the conversation brings you to the connection. At the appropriate time, inquire about fear or one of the other hidden companions of pride.

THE FAILURE OF FEAR AND PRIDE

Roots provide strength for a tree—to help the tree stand firm against the fierce attack of stormy weather. Likewise, people live in fear and respond with pride in an attempt to withstand the weak soil of insecurity. However, these roots support a false sense of security. The storms of life expose the weakness of our faulty system. When one root fails to strengthen us, we turn to the other and redouble our efforts, entering into further bondage.

Fear is a universal human experience. Fear arrived hot on the heels of Adam and Eve's first sin of pride and rebellion and fear is a result of our pride as well as our independence. Now it is a good thing for a person to overcome their fears and not be subject to them. Often, someone who has a fear of flying will deliberately fly in an airplane to overcome that fear. Or one who is terrified of public speaking may take a course in speech or join Toastmasters. If someone comes to us for prayer, however, we want to get to the root of fear. Even though a particular expression of fear has been overcome, that does not mean the axe has been laid to the root. The taproot of a large tree is almost impossible to dig out; without the help of the Holy Spirit, it is impossible to rid ourselves of fear—we will simply swap one fear for another that we find more acceptable. So what root needs to be hacked apart and carted off? The root of pride.

I once ministered to a young woman who told me she grew up as the good child, the favorite. Her identity was found in being the one Mom approved of who did not get in trouble and who did the right thing. One day when her mom was beginning a relationship with a man (her parents were divorced), her mother unjustly accused her of stealing. This cut to her core. She had spent her whole life working to keep the rules and gain her mom's (and God's) approval. She was proud of her record and felt secure because of it. She would do anything to keep her good standing in the family. Her deep fear of rejection flared up. Later that day, she shoplifted for the first time. Since she was not experienced, she was caught. Now she had a criminal record—and she had added guilt, shame, and embarrassment to the fear of rejection that was now exposed and raw. I was able to tell her that at some point every perfectionist fails. No one can ever be good enough to overcome insecurity and fear of rejection. And it is not unusual for one who is driven to be perfect to dramatically crash and find themselves caught by something that is a total contradiction to the way they previously lived.

I helped her to see how pride and insecurity held her in bondage in conjunction with the other things she shared in the interview. For the first time, she understood that her struggle was not only with herself but also with a diabolical plan to destroy her. In her pride, she had traded the fear of rejection for the perfectionism and legalism, but as she named her enemies and broke their power in renunciations, victory came. Because she learned how to continue to face her enemies using the Five Keys, she can walk in freedom.

This young woman had attempted to cover her nakedness by being as perfect as she could be. Others try to hide by taking a superior position through judgments, criticism, and accusations. No matter how much we try to overcome our exposure as deeply flawed people, we will fail. If we medicate ourselves through drugs or pornography or other addictive behaviors (all attempts to save ourselves), we will fail. This failure will lead to deeper isolation and loneliness, for our efforts will never be good enough to overcome the God-sized hole in our hearts.

Nothing we do will ever be good enough to take away our suspicion that there is something wrong with us. The effort to be perfect is too much. Someday we will give up, our unredeemed selves will be exposed, and we will see what a wretch we are apart from grace. Often others will see it too, as in the case of the young woman mentioned above.

Many people come to us because they have crashed and are overwhelmed by their failures. They are disillusioned and humiliated by failure and are now bombarded with negative thoughts: hopelessness, purposelessness, self-rejection, self-hatred, fear of the future or the past, fear of embarrassment or further rejection—all these and more can come on like a stampeding herd.

The Trunk and Branches—Lies and Sinful Behaviors

The roots of fear and pride, driven by insecurity, draw deeply from the swamp, which is the power of sin working in our lives. Decay and death give rise to the trunk, which represents our perceptions and reactions to the experiences of life. This trunk is on the surface and visible, and here we see that fear and pride give rise to rejection and abandonment. Let us examine the trunk to see how the sinful nature interacts with the events of life.

When Jesus hung on the cross, identifying Himself with our sin, our condition of alienation from God, He cried out from the depths of this human experience, "Eli, Eli, la'ma sabach-tha'ni?" That is, "My God, My God, why hast Thou forsaken Me?" (Matthew 27:46). His cry expressed the condition of the human heart. Deep-seated fear and insecurity give rise to feelings of rejection and abandonment that then are confirmed by life's experiences. These experiences reveal the deeper human condition of man's alienation from God because of our sin.

Parents have misrepresented God to their children since the beginning. Even when they represent God's love rightly, a child may still interpret this love wrongly because of their sinful nature. Instead of realizing their need for a redeemer to save them, they may blame others or themselves. Ultimately, they may blame God. Without the revelation of His Son, the growing child becomes an adult who says things like, "How can I believe in a good God when He allows such evil?" Or he resents and rejects Him, saying bitterly, "Where was God when I needed Him?" Or, based on the emptiness within, he declares, "I am alone in this universe; after death there is nothing." This young adult now imagines God based on their experiences instead of understanding the God who reveals Himself. He imagines God as one who needs to be appeased: "I have to earn His love" or "I do not know what He wants." Sometimes a child may imagine God as their "teddy bear God" who will always be there to comfort them when they need comfort. They will have little, if any, expectations of God beyond that and will believe He has little expectations of them. What is wrong with the views of God that are born out of our human experience and come from our imagination? In each case, we remain at the center; we remain God's equal (or even His master). That means the sin of Adam continues.

From the roots and trunk, the branches are formed. As we have seen, the branches on this tree are the twisted thoughts, lies, and deceptive thinking that give a place for evil spirits to rest. Some branches push outward; others seek the shade. How does this work in a person's life? If I find during an interview that there was anger, violence, or arguing in the home, I will often ask, "What did you do when your parents fought?" The answers are very revealing. If the individual got angry, tried to get in the middle, hated Mom or Dad, or fantasized about defending Mom, I see their reactions as branches that push outward. If they express that they were afraid or hid in some way by escaping into reading or into their room, or if they blamed themselves, I see their reactions as branches that seek the shade. They want to remain obscured. The first reaction comes from aggression based on pride and the need to control, the second from withdrawal based on fear.

Another Tree—Our Nature in Christ

The tree I described above is that of the sinful nature. But a believer has been given a new nature in Christ (see Figure B). The revelation of the Father who sends His Son is radically different from the twisted view of God we create based on our human experience alone. Our life in Christ is represented by a tree planted by the water of life. Jeremiah describes us this way: "He is like a tree planted by water, that sends out its roots by the stream, and does not fear when heat comes, for its

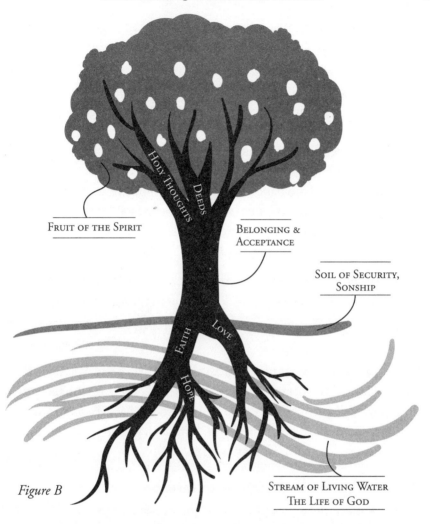

Figure B

leaves remain green, and is not anxious in the year of drought, for it does not cease to bear fruit" (Jeremiah 17:8).

The power of sin is not flowing through this tree anymore. The old sinful nature, no longer drawing up death and decay from the swamp of sin, is dried up, like a tree with its roots cut out. Our redeemed self, the self that is crucified and raised with Christ, draws living water and is therefore insecure no longer. This stream of living water represents our new nature united to Christ and sharing communion with God. We share in the love of God the Father, who is love itself. Our identity is now firmly established as a son or daughter of the eternal Father, and in this reality we are secure.

The power of God flows through the twin roots of love and faith (from which hope is born) and produces acceptance and assurance of our place in God's kingdom. Throughout our lives, faith and love are expressed in the lovely branches of holy thoughts and deeds, which carry the Spirit's fruit. Now we can interpret life through the truth of God's Word. You see, these branches represent a completely new way of thinking: the mind does not agree anymore with lies but agrees only with the truth of God's revelation in His Word.

When the one who has come for prayer renounces the lie and agrees with God's spoken Word, they will be transformed by the renewal of their mind (Romans 12:2). They will be able to hold on to their freedom by learning to think in agreement with the truth.

> *Finally, brethren, whatever is true, whatever is honorable, whatever is just, whatever is pure, whatever is lovely, whatever is gracious, if there is any excellence, if there is anything worthy of praise, think about these things.*
>
> Philippians 4:8

Thinking on what is pure and excellent will give rise to actions that God will bless. The personality and the works of the one who has come for prayer will be marked by the fruit of the Spirit. "But the fruit of the Spirit is love, joy, peace, patience, kindness, goodness, faithfulness, gentleness, self-control" (Galatians 5:22-23).

The Door to Freedom

God offers freedom. His freedom comes by grace through His Son. By grace, humiliation leads to humility and fear turns to love. Many times people are brought comfort in their pain through their faith, but they are not delivered. Some learn through counseling to manage their issues and are no longer overwhelmed by them. This is good. We give thanks. But we cannot dilute the power of the Good News. Jesus wants to cut to the root and set us free. This is the message we carry! Believers are children of an eternal Father who has never rejected or abandoned them. Instead, Jesus made a way for us and each of us enters the Father's heart by grace. Not any of our willfulness, pride, and effort will enable us to enter the door. Only grace. The empowering presence of God welcomes us when we stop grasping for what we need and simply ask—knocking on the only door that leads to freedom. Jesus alone is the door of escape, the door to the heart of the Father: The Spirit of Christ Himself makes each believer willing to bow their neck and renounce the pride and rebellion that have characterized their life. You have been entrusted with the power of the gospel that brings light and understanding to those who are walking in darkness. It is your privilege to help bring liberty to those who are oppressed.

Chapter 8
Self-Justification

I have been crucified with Christ; it is no longer I who live, but Christ who lives in me; and the life I now live in the flesh I live by faith in the Son of God, who loved me and gave Himself for me. (GALATIANS 2:20)

Adam and Eve knew they were in trouble as soon as they ate the forbidden fruit. The serpent was right—with the first bite and swallow, their eyes were opened and they knew both good and evil in a way they had never known before. They now had a choice: throw themselves upon the mercy of the loving Father who had walked and talked with them in the cool of the day or find some other way to respond to this new reality. They chose to hide, to cover themselves with fig leaves, and to blame each other and the serpent. They chose self-justification.

Self-justification has been the default response of sinful man ever since. The Bible teaches that we are *justified* by God (vindicated, pronounced "not guilty," and restored to divine sonship) only by grace through our faith in the work of Jesus Christ on the cross. Self-justification, however, is an insidious deception. How many of us have lived in ways that do not line up with our beliefs? How many of us live our lives under legalism, striving to believe God accepts us when Mom and Dad never did? How many of us misunderstand the teaching of our church and think we can get to heaven if only we are good enough, go to church enough, or keep the commandments well enough? As you minister using the UNBOUND model, you will encounter self-justification again and again. As you do, you may even recognize it at work in your own life.

Deception

Self-justification is the deception that we can be good enough to deserve God's love and blessing or we can earn His acceptance by keeping the rules. While cooperating with God's grace in doing good works is necessary (James 2:17), it is a deception to think being good is the basis for belonging to the kingdom of God. Our eternal life is based on the saving work of Christ—His death, His resurrection, and His sending of the Holy Spirit. Like Adam and Eve, we need to throw ourselves on the Lord's mercy, but we tend to plaster on fig leaves as well. Self-justification leads us to make the case that "I am okay; I am not so bad." It leads us to compare ourselves to others ("I am better than her.") or to start listing our merits ("I tithe," "I serve," "I…") The fig leaves of blame, excuses, explanations, judgment, and comparison make for fragile clothes. When we keep the rules, we can trust in the love of God, but when we fail, we feel forsaken.

Since no one likes to feel forsaken, people will perform amazing contortions with their minds in order to hide their sin from themselves. I remember a married man I talked to once who looked the flight attendant of our plane up and down. When the conversation got around to God, he made the case that he was a good person and expected to go to heaven. He did not mess around with other women—too much. Yes, he implied he had committed adultery, but he was better than others he knew and better than he could have been if he let himself go. I was once no different. Even as a young boy, I consoled myself over my concern that I might not be good enough to go to heaven by thinking, "Maybe I am not good enough to go to heaven, but at least I am better than Louie."

Who Is Good?

We self-justify because we want to be good. A man came up to Jesus and said: "'Good Teacher, what must I do to inherit eternal life?' And Jesus said to him, 'Why do you call Me good? No one is good but God alone'" (Mark 10:17-18). Jesus was not denying He was good; He was challenging the man to understand that all goodness comes from God—it comes to us as a gift. Jesus is indeed good. He was without sin and He was never separated from His Father. Our goodness exists only because we share His goodness through our faith in Him. "Doing good" is an expression of being good, which is only possible by the grace of union with the One who is good.

During one UNBOUND interview, I listed a number of things for the man to renounce. As we came to the end of the interview, he realized I had quite a long list. He looked over at me. "I am really not that bad," he said. Because of the rapport we had developed in the session, I could say to him, "I guess we should add self-justification to the list." We both laughed, but it was true. God revealed his heart, which is what this man wanted. As you minister, you may hear "I'm not that bad" often. Many people are so afraid of being judged, so fearful of the deep insecurity that is provoked when they share their junk, that they are quick to self-justify in this way. You can understand this fear. At the same time, it is important to help each person see that when they come before the Lord to be set free, they need to recognize that apart from their union with Christ, they really are a sinner who is lost; they really are capable of all kinds of evil. All of us are. All the self-justification in the world will not change this reality.

You may have heard someone attempt to encourage someone else by saying,

"Do not be discouraged; you are such a good person." Really? If you have ever had someone say something like this to you, you know it does not work. It hasn't worked for you and it won't work for the one to whom you minister. They may take momentary encouragement from such words, but such statements will not produce what you intend. These words will not free them, nor will they build their faith. They are words that do not stick. We all know we are not very good or faithful. They know it; you know it. We certainly know we are not deserving of the sacrificial death of Jesus. If we try to stand before God based on how good we are, we will fail every time.

In fact, when the apostle Paul looked back at his sinful past, he did not make a defense based upon his zealousness for the law or his ignorance of the truth. Rather, he delighted in the fact that his former life demonstrated how wide and deep is the mercy of God.

> *...Christ Jesus came into the world to save sinners. And I am the foremost of sinners; but I received mercy for this reason, that in me, as the foremost, Jesus Christ might display His perfect patience for an example to those who were to believe in Him for eternal life.*
>
> 1 Timothy 1:15b-16

The truth is that whatever good any believer has done was done by the grace of God. Their failures, their sins, are simply a revelation of the human heart apart from His grace and mercy. So do not offer false encouragement. Instead, look for a sign of God's goodness in their lives. Recognize the grace of God at work and speak increase and a fuller surrender to the gift of God. Smile at the believer with delight because you see the hand of God bringing them to deeper faith and trust.

RECOGNIZING SELF-JUSTIFICATION

The greatest lessons I have learned about people have come from the process of listening and leading people to renounce their enemies and take hold of their freedom. Years ago, I prayed for a lawyer whose fear and anxiety just refused to leave. A lot of his anxiety had to do with work. We had already covered rejection and father issues, so I asked him what went through his mind while at work. He said when he sat at his desk, he was always ready to explain how he was using his time. No one ever asked, but he was always ready. This was more than a simple explanation; this was a defense. The possibility of being asked represented an attack. When he renounced self-justification, he experienced freedom. I never forgot that lesson. Insecurity and fear lead to pride. Pride is often expressed as self-justification. His testimony is instructive:

> I can testify that I am a new man since Saturday! Since I have returned to work on Monday, I have been able to just do my work without feeling this terrible sense that I am doing the wrong thing or spending too much time or obsessing about getting my quota of billable hours in the day. Oddly, I have had moments when I have had a twinge of a familiar old feeling of being on the wrong track,

and then it "disappears." I don't really have to do or say anything to make it go away.

After receiving your e-mail, I thought of another example of the self-justification spirit I have lived with at times in the past. When I started my current job, ten years ago, I had a very clear plan that no one would ever be able to say I hadn't tried hard enough. I would fill Monday through Saturday working so I wouldn't feel any guilt that I wasn't doing enough. Of course, I was exhausted and filled with bitterness and I had a big chip on my shoulder. I stopped doing that about five years ago after my first taste of healing. But, as you saw on Saturday, there was a lot left.

As you can see, self-justification sometimes shows up as striving, but at other times, it is recognized by the inability to forgive oneself. I commonly ask people if they believe God has forgiven them. If they have doubts about it, I will inquire further and ask about guilt, shame, or condemnation. But I have also learned to ask if they have forgiven themselves. If they are confused about what that would look like, I may ask them about self-criticism, self-condemnation, and the like, which are built upon the foundation of pride. Many people believe firmly that God has forgiven them but they cannot forgive themselves. They may say, "How could I have been so stupid?" or "I can't believe I did that." This too is self-justification. This self-justification comes from the pride that wants to be good enough to be deserving rather than forgiven and loved. When they declare, "In the name of Jesus I forgive myself for being so stupid when I…" and then renounce unforgiveness and any other of the "self" sins they have fallen prey to, they can receive a deep sense of liberation.

Another form of self-justification is the need to excuse. I once prayed with a young Catholic believer. I asked him if he knew what self-justification was. He said no. After I started to describe it, he interrupted me. "I know what you mean. Every time I go to the priest to confess my sin, I find I cannot just confess my sins; I compulsively have to explain them." Bingo. He got it. Any time we defend, explain, blame others, or make excuses for our moral failures, we are in the grasp of self-justification.

Discouragement often results from self-justification. When circumstances do not work out well for us, we are vulnerable to guilt and condemnation, which are accompanied by lies such as, "I am no good." If we are convinced we are acceptable to God and others based upon our own righteousness (right living), then our defenses will crumble when we fail to meet our standards. When our own righteousness fails, when it no longer does what we rely on it to do, we are left with companions like discouragement, self-doubt, self-rejection, and self-judgment.

Here is another way self-justification operates in us: we love in order to get. Once I prayed with a man whose wife was present during the session. I felt led to ask him if he struggled with pride. He smiled sheepishly and said, "No, not really. Everyone considers me a humble guy." His wife nodded her head in agreement. I quickly crossed pride off the notes I was making. Later in the interview, I asked him if he knew what self-justification meant. He said no. When I described it, the light bulb went on. He was driven to be the nice guy everyone liked. That drive to look good and look humble was a cover for the deeper need for acceptance that was being sought through self-justification. When I asked him if he understood the relationship to pride, he immediately saw the connection. Sometimes we only see pride as it is expressed in arrogance or superiority rather than as an expression of unworthiness—or insecurity or a need for reassurance. Self-justification can be a means of protecting ourselves from rejection. This self-protection keeps us from loving as Jesus loved. We love not to give but to get our own needs met.

Exposing the Enemy

Self-justification finds a home among the various expressions of pride I wrote about in the last chapter. Take a moment now to read over the list of names below. As you read, be aware that evil spirits will feed off each other. See if you can make a connection between any of these and self-justification.

Self-rejection, self-judgment, legalism, self-blame, self-condemnation, religiosity (focus on outward appearances and the external practice of the faith), lying, stubbornness, blame, criticism, judgment, self-reliance, independence, guilt, self-accusation and shame. Also, self-protection, insistence on being right, fear of God's wrath, fear of rejection. Related spirits are pride, self-righteousness, insecurity, unworthiness, guilt, condemnation, comparison, aloneness, isolation.

If you do not see the connection just yet, you will. As you pray for people and listen to their stories, God will open your understanding to the interrelationship of the enemy's strategies and lies. You will learn about the connections one by one in a way you will remember. For now it is good enough to know what self-justification is and that the interrelationship of lies that come with pride builds a stronghold for the enemy to inhabit.

I have seen what self-justification has done in others' lives as well as in my own. It is a way of hiding from our absolute need for God. It will always keep us far from God. Unless self-justification is exposed, the thief will have robbed the believer of their deepest joy and in very real ways, they will be in bondage to the evil one. Fortunately, God has provided a way of escape, a way to defeat this enemy in all its forms. The way is accepting *God's* vindication of us, a vindication that comes "from God alone, for Christ's sake, by grace, through faith in 'the gospel of God's Son'" (Romans 1:1-3).[1]

CHRIST'S GREAT LOVE

One of the lines from John Mark McMillan's song *How He Loves Us* goes, "I do not have time to think about regrets when I think about how He loves me." This line pierces my heart every time. His love, understood through the atoning sacrifice of Jesus, removes our need to justify ourselves, to redeem ourselves, to compare ourselves, to explain ourselves. False guilt, condemnation, and regrets lose their power to torment us. "He himself bore our sins in his body on the tree, that we might die to sin and live to righteousness. By his wounds, you have been healed" (1 Peter 2:24).

---

[1] *Joint Declaration on the Doctrine of Justification*, Pontifical Council for Promoting Christian Unity and the Lutheran World Federation, 1999. Other Protestant denominations identify this truth as *sola fide* and *sola gratia*. Much ink and even some blood have been spilled over the doctrine of God's justification. All Christians agree, however, that "Christ Himself is our righteousness."

We are justified through Christ and now have a place without shame before the eternal Father. Think of the freedom that comes with the simple recognition that the work has been done on our behalf. Jesus died for us while we were still in our sins and God's love for us will never waver. As we receive His justification by grace, we can confess our sins without an explanation. We no longer need to fear God's wrath.

If you minister to someone who is trapped by self-justification, it may be they have never encountered the transforming power of the love of God in Jesus, His Son. They may be most aware of God's wrath toward their sin. Yes, God does have wrath toward sin; if a person has hardened their heart and identified with the sin God hates, they come under that wrath. But Scripture says, "Perfect loves casts out fear" (1 John 4:18) and the Father's love is perfect. If the one to whom you minister will receive the Savior and identify with the Son, they will find that God the Father is always the father of the prodigal. God provides shelter under the wings of the Almighty (Psalm 91). The believer can find peace with God as they accept Jesus, who was the perfect offering for sin. Not fearing punishment, now they will be able to humble themselves and honestly confess their sins. They will have no more need of self-justification, for they will know they are cleansed not only from that sin but also from all unrighteousness (1 John 1:9).

It may be that freedom will come from the first of the Five Keys as you lead a person in a prayer of surrender to Christ. Or they may be loosed from bondage to self-justification as they name and renounce spirits related to pride and insecurity. As you pray with an individual, remember to look for interrelationships: insecurity and fear are doorways to pride. Fear of hell, fear of God's wrath, and fear of God's rejection are all insecurities born out of the consequences of living under the power of sin in a fallen world. Any one of these may lead to self-justification and self-righteousness. Then again, they might need to forgive someone who has misrepresented God to them, someone who left an enduring negative mark of fear on their life. It is likely that all three keys–repentance and faith, forgiveness, and renunciation–will be needed to break the hold of self-justification.

Self-Justification

PRAYING FOR OTHERS

Understanding self-justification and that our standing before God comes from Him by alone will profoundly affect how you pray the Father's blessing. Do not look to heaven and say, "Lord, bless John. He is such a good man; he is a wonderful father and so deserving of Your love." John will know this is not true. He will know his goodness is not his own doing and his goodness will never be adequate. (If he thinks it is adequate, he is deceived.) He may be grateful for your thoughts, but your words will not bring the blessing of God into his life. Nor will it bless him to say, "John is a miserable worm, unworthy of a drop of your love." In truth, if you focus on God and what the Father has revealed in the Son, you will speak words that are a true blessing. As you focus on the work of the Holy Spirit in John's life, you will be able to speak to his heart. You will be able to pray with gratitude for what God has revealed and what he desires to bring to life in John. You will be able to give thanks for the grace that has been evident in his life and ask God for an increase of His blessing, which He gives so freely to those who come to Him.

Justification is at the heart of what Jesus has done for us. This is the foundation from which we for pray for the Father's blessing for others and ourselves. We bring people before the throne of the Father because of what Jesus has done. They belong because the Son of God dwells in them, making them worthy to enter the throne room and sit at His table or climb onto His lap. In the next chapter, I will share with you some practical ways of praying the Father's blessing that will bring healing and restoration.

May the meditations of your heart give you words that communicate these truths.

CHAPTER 9
Speaking the Father's Blessing

God has sent the Spirit of his Son into our hearts, crying, "Abba! Father!" (GALATIANS 4:6)

At a conference, a woman approached me and asked if she could read me something from UNBOUND that touched her. She read the following passage from page 206:

> If there is anything I wish to grow in, it is the ability to speak blessing into someone's life. I long to be able, by the power of the Spirit, to discern the area of deepest need and speak something that God sees in the person, something at the core of his being that he understands and knows but has yet to own, because it has never been spoken. As you pray for people, be open to the Holy Spirit revealing their hearts to you so you can bring blessing to their identities and destinies. Always remember the Father is passionate to bless His children. Sometimes we just have to get out of the way and ask God to speak to them.

As she read these words, I was deeply moved. *Yes. Yes*, I thought, *this is still my desire. I want to grow in speaking blessings into the hearts of people by the power of the Holy Spirit*. People often embrace freedom at the moment they are blessed! Everything we do in UNBOUND ministry leads to the fifth key, the blessing of the Father. As we lead a person through the first four keys, Jesus comes into their temple, overthrows the tables, drives out their enemies that defile the dwelling place of the Almighty Father, and claims their heart as a place for intimacy with

God—a place for the Lord's presence. Now they have ears to hear the words of blessing the Father has whispered to them their entire life. Now they know the Father runs to them, has always been running to them, just as the prodigal's father ran to greet him while he was still far off.

Sometimes those who minister use the Five Keys and pray for a person to be blessed and filled with God's love but fall short of entering into the power of speaking the Father's blessings. Since the Father is the truth that Jesus wants to reveal, and since the Father reveals our identity, Jesus' work is not done until He leads us to the Father, until we encounter Him as the Son, and until the Holy Spirit is released to cry from our depths, "Abba! Father." Be aware of all three persons of the Trinity as you speak the Father's blessing. Let me give you some practical helps in speaking the Father's blessing.

KNOW YOUR OWN PLACE FIRST

Your ability to speak the Father's blessing begins with your own relationship with the Father through the Son. You must have your own history of talking to Him, receiving from Him, and knowing that in Christ you have been made righteous and have a place before the Father as His son or daughter. As you have received the gift of sonship from Jesus, so you can look at the person before you, recognize Jesus dwelling in them, and speak from the Father's heart the blessing they have longed for.

STAND AS ONE JOINED TO CHRIST

After you lead the person through the first four keys, have them stand up for the Father's blessing. This shifts the atmosphere and marks the beginning of the blessing. It is no longer a time of struggle. That is over; now is a time to receive. Therefore, stand before the Father. No one can stand before the glory of God except those who come to Him joined to the Son. So by standing, you and the person are saying they have been made worthy by the blood of the Lamb to enter into the presence of the King of Kings, Lord of Lords, who they know as Abba, Papa God. This is as true for you as it is for the one who came for prayer.

Know Who You Trust

As you begin to pray, trust the Holy Spirit to lead you. Pause for a moment and look at the person, expecting you will be able to see and know the Father's heart. Do not worry about what you will say. Call to mind the Father who ran to the returning prodigal, and know this is a moment the Father has been waiting for. The person before you has cast off their false identity and is coming home as the Father's son or daughter in Christ. Expect to be surprised by the words you speak on God's behalf. Do not let your words or lack of words become a distraction. Offer what you have. Sometimes little is big. Sometimes anointed words will flow and other times you may have little to say and you may just stand in awe as the presence of God falls upon the person. Always keep your eyes open and your heart turned to God. Actively listen to the Holy Spirit. There have been times I have just had the person sit again and I have sat in silence with them for five or ten minutes as God visited His child. One time I actually left the room and came back thirty minutes later. Always follow the leading of the Spirit. The Spirit searches the mind and the heart and knows just what the person needs.

Remember the Truth

God reveals truth in His Word; the Holy Spirit reveals truth to the heart. A good place to start as you bless someone is by remembering the truth God has revealed.

- Jesus the Son dwells in every believer. It is His work to lead him to the Father. Some people have always known God as Jesus the Savior and have not encountered the Father. Now that their dads and moms have been forgiven and the lies have been renounced, they are free to follow Jesus to the Father's house.

- The Holy Spirit dwells in every believer and the Spirit wants to go to the very depth of the person's being and cry out from that place to the Father, "Abba, my Father."

- The Father is already running to the person and is ready to embrace them and restore to them their true identity as a child—a son or daughter of God.

SPEAK THE BLESSING

Blessings need to be spoken. The Father is ready to reveal Himself and bring His blessing. The words we speak reveal the reality of what God is doing and will be an instrument God uses to enable the person to acknowledge and receive His grace.

What should you say? My wife Janet has learned to start by saying, "The Father says…" and then she yields to the heart of the Father and speaks into the person's heart. Sometimes she gets images and other times the words just seem to flow. During the session, the person has revealed himself or herself to you. You know them more than you may think. Speak from your heart and the Lord will bring out of you the blessings that meet the needs of the heart.

I usually wait a moment for the Lord to show me where to begin. Sometimes a new image comes to mind. Other times God brings me images He has given me in the past or words He has used to penetrate the depths of a person's heart and bring liberation. I share with you some of the ways I have been led to pray, not that you would memorize them and try to reproduce them but simply as an example for you. It is my hope that my examples will encourage you to receive the Father's heart from the Father Himself so you can speak words that bring life. Let the Holy Spirit use your imagination to lead you to see things that bring revealed truth to life in unique ways.

1. As I do at every conference, I may choose to bring a person again to that place of baptism, to union with Jesus in the Jordan, and speak over them the words of the Scriptures. "This is my son; this is my daughter with whom I am well pleased–in whom I take great delight or great pleasure."

2. Sometimes in my mind's eye I see Jesus walking with a child or Jesus carrying a child. At other times, He is with an adult, walking down a wooded path to a house hidden in the woods. As they approach, the one with Jesus discovers it is the Father's house. Jesus may show the way to an open door or He may open the door, but the person needs to willingly step over the threshold into the Father's presence. In the house, the Father is waiting. Every person responds differently to the Father. One will run to embrace the Father; another

will climb on His lap. One will sit at the table with the Father's loving gaze on them. Still another will spill their milk and hear the Father laugh with joy because He knows their heart and has never stopped looking at their heart (It can be very liberating for a recovering perfectionist to spill their milk on the beautiful table and know it is okay to mess up in the Father's house).

3. On occasion I see the one I pray with dressed in white. They wear a beautiful gown and Jesus escorts them to the majestic throne room of God. There they allow the Father to look at and delight in their beauty.

4. Sometimes I see a young man (or woman) at a track or at a baseball or soccer field. The Father is in the stands shouting their name and saying, "That is My son (My daughter)." He does so without reservation as He proudly identifies with this person and gives them the strength and confidence to succeed. The Father never missed one game! He saw every pitch, every goal!

5. I have had similar pictures for adults. The race is about to begin, or perhaps the person is already running the race, and the Father stands up for them to let them know they will finish the race and not falter. Once, as I looked closer at a similar picture, I realized there was only one person in the stadium stands. The race about to be run would be run for just that one, the One who is faithful and true.

6. I might be aware of the moment of the person's conception and see the Father look at them and smile with delight. The Father may have bragged to the angels about this little one. He spoke their name long before their parents named them. One time I had the image of God speaking a person's name and I had the sense of her name resounding through the universe, bouncing off the stars and echoing everywhere. The Father was the first to speak her name. He knew her true identity. When I have these kinds of pictures, I might make a declaration that the Father watched over them in the womb and protected them and on the day they were born the Father danced over them; He held them high for all to see.

Other times the Father weeps over them, knowing what they would have to suffer, but He knows the end from the beginning and He sent His very own Son to suffer and die for them, to take their place and save them.

When I see an image, I speak it aloud into the person's life, for pictures stick more than words for many people. You will find that the person is often helped as you learn to pray out of images. But the Lord, the Word, also sends inspired words that cut to the core. These words may be very simple, such as:

7. A prayer for the Spirit to be released, to cry out, "Abba, Father" from within them or a prayer for the person to be free to identify with the living Lord Jesus, who dwells within them, sharing with them His divine Sonship.

8. A prayer such as, "In the name of Jesus, I speak into your heart the blessing of the Father, who has always loved you, desired you. He wanted you to come to life. He has seen your heart and He has never rejected you. When you were conceived, He took great delight as He breathed life into you."

9. A parent's prayer of blessing such as, "As a father and on behalf of the heavenly Father, I bless you as a man, I bless your decisions, I bless you as a father and a husband. I declare that you have what it takes, you will finish the race, and one day you will hear the words you long to hear: 'Well done, My good and faithful servant.'" Or "As a father and on behalf of the heavenly Father, I bless you as a woman; I bless your personality, your body, your features; I bless you as a mother and wife. I bless you with freedom that Jesus has given you and I say, 'Increase.' God wants to see your beauty. Lord, increase her freedom so that all may see her beauty."

These prayers may be simple, but they are so powerful for the ones who have never heard their mom or dad bless their identity or their destiny. Just as I speak as a father, Janet might bless from her authority as a mother who listens to the heart of the Father. She may say, "As a mother, I bless your personality, your emotions, your features, your plans, your compassion…"

Following a moment of release, you may be filled with thousands of good words. It is important to pause and let the good things you are filled with settle so you can choose something that speaks to the heart. Once you have, go for it and trust the Lord will lead you. You do not need a lot of words. A few simple words that speak to the heart are much better than a multiplicity of words spilling out of you.

You cannot pray effectively without the help of the Holy Spirit. Some people are not quite ready to come to the Father and you cannot compel them by forcing an image. Keep your eyes open so you can sense if you are leading the person down the path to the Father's heart. If you are unsure, stop and ask if they are sensing anything or seeing anything.

Some people have always called God "Father," but now they will encounter Him more deeply. Some have a relationship with the Father but have never connected in a deeply personal way with Jesus—and now they will, as the Father introduces them to His Son. Others may need Jesus to breathe on them the Holy Spirit, who will release them to come to the Father.

THE BLESSING AS PROPHECY

I have always considered these kinds of images and words as prophetic, especially the first time I received them. When God impresses them on my heart to use again, I believe they are inspired. The more you carry from past encounters with the Lord, the easier it is for the Holy Spirit to inspire you as you pray. Prophecy and inspired words are meant to be encouragement. They do not need to be spoken as if you are delivering information. Prophecy is the heartbeat of God, the now Word spoken into a heart. Speak with passion or an attitude that conveys the Word you are bringing. At the same time, do it in a way that offers the Word but does not force it. Keep your eyes open, recognizing that otherwise you may miss the heart of what the Holy Spirit is saying or that what you say may be misinterpreted.

Sometimes, after I pray the Father's blessing at a conference, the spiritual atmosphere is so thick with the presence of God that it is easy to quickly see or hear from God things I can offer as a blessing. Often I am very tired at the end of the last session. Nothing in me feels alert or sensitive to God's voice. But if I ask Him and think of His desire to bless and look with compassion on those who come, He amazes me with what I find myself saying.

It is always a blessing when God speaks through me a word that allows the person to know God has heard their prayer, that He knows and sees them. It may happen that after I share an image I see, I find out they saw the same thing before I spoke. When that happens, replace with: faith in God's personal love comes to life.

Let me share a few stories from my years of praying the Father's blessing. One time as I touched a woman I was about to pray for at the end of the conference, I saw an image of a strawberry patch with someone leaning over it. I said, "I do not know what it means, but I see a child picking strawberries." The woman's whole countenance changed; it was filled with gratitude. She said, "My grandmother was the only person who nurtured me and she was the one who took me to pick strawberries." I knew what to declare: "Your grandmother was a vessel of the Father's love for you. He was there revealing Himself to you."

As I began a session for a young woman, I immediately got a picture of Jesus giving her a huge box with a ribbon on it. Often I will wait for the interview and the appropriate time to share what I saw. But on this day I said, "Do you like surprise presents?" She said, "Oh yes!" I described what I saw. As I interviewed her, I found she was a victim of incest and a great deal of rejection. As I prayed the Father's blessing at the end, I got a glimpse of what was in the box. Jesus had brought her a beautiful white wedding dress that was hers to wear before the Father. Jesus had restored her purity and given her victory. She shared in His righteousness.

God can bring any image to mind. Once you are in God's presence, allow yourself to see things through your imagination. You may get strange pictures and you can simply say, "I have a strange picture." After you reveal the image, ask, "Does it mean anything to you?" The important thing to remember is the image is secondary to what it represents. Pay attention to the presence of God that is revealed through the prayer or the image. Often, as you begin to share the image, you will start to get insight into what God wants to impart. Then you can just pray or declare what it is you have received, such as:

"God has seen you as you whispered to Him every night. He has seen your tears that have fallen on your pillow."

"He sees you as someone who has a servant's heart."

"God sees your courage; you are a rock that others can rely on. This gives the Father great pleasure."

I share this, fully aware that not every one of you will get pictures or images. Many of you will have Scriptures or thoughts based on what God has spoken to you in the past come to mind. The Holy Spirit can guide you not only to quote the Scripture but also to impart the meaning as you speak into the heart. You may find it is simpler just to pray that Jesus would lead the individual you are praying with to the Father's heart. Then wait on the Holy Spirit and gently ask if they are sensing/feeling/seeing anything. Then you can speak based on what they tell you and what God brings to your mind. Remember that God can and will use you and your prayers even if you do not feel they are inspired. Of course, you will need to grow in being a vessel of the Father's blessings, but it will always remain His work.

Symbols in God's Kingdom

Images can be brought into your mind from Bible verses you know or from the world around you. I sometimes see symbols of freedom such as open fields with brilliant light from the sun or fields with a cool breeze blowing the flowers. A child dancing with the Father or a child running and laughing with their dad are also symbols of freedom. The Scriptures are full of word pictures. In Luke 15, Jesus describes joy in heaven when He says, "Just so, I tell you, there will be more joy in heaven over one sinner who repents than over ninety-nine righteous persons who need no repentance." We can all visualize the party—the cheering, the clapping, and the dancing—that accompanies one sinner's repentance. As you remember your Scripture, God can lead you to speak a blessing that communicates the Father's rejoicing with the angels over the person's conception or birth or this day of liberation.

As one who prays for others using the UNBOUND model, you can be confident the Holy Spirit is eager to restore the identity of each of

His children. Your words, your pictures come from Him as you seek the Father's presence. When you speak from the Father's heart, you are mediating His presence to the man or woman who has come for liberation. This man's destiny, this woman's purpose, is the same as yours—to know that the Father is present and to know the reality of the promise He spoke to Moses: "I will be with you."

May the Father bless you and allow you by the power of the Spirit to discern the area of deepest need and speak something God sees in the person. May you speak something at the core of their being that they understand and know but have yet to own because it has never been spoken.

PART III
MAKING SENSE OF UNBOUND:
Frequently Asked Questions

As we travel to many different cities and countries, Janet and I repeatedly encounter the same questions. Although most of the questions have already been carefully answered in UNBOUND and *Resisting the Devil*, some questions are worth considering in this new format since they come from people who have been in ministry and who are having a difficult time understanding the differences between the UNBOUND model and the approach they were using in the past. Other questions arise because leaders are inexperienced and encounter a difficult situation for the first time.

I am very grateful for the many people who have been tirelessly serving the Lord and His people in deliverance ministry. They have been pioneers, opening the door so others, like me, can develop in their ability to help men and women find freedom in Christ. While it is true I have studied and reflected on many different approaches to deliverance, and while I continually test and question what I have learned in light of the wisdom gained by those who came before, I do not pretend to be an expert on these other practices. I write this guidebook not to argue for my way above others but to clarify my teaching for those who have embraced the UNBOUND model of deliverance prayer. Of course, I would be delighted if my explanations and reflections led others to examine their ministry in a new way, but that is not my purpose here. Rather, I write primarily for the benefit of those who have read *UNBOUND: A Practical Guide to Deliverance* and who understand the

Five Keys taught within that book—keys which merge inner healing with non-confrontational deliverance from the influence of evil spirits.

Chapter 10 covers questions that relate to your personal growth as a leader. Chapter 11 deals specifically with issues that arise in ministry. Chapter 12 answers concerns raised by those who have experience with other models of healing and deliverance.

List of Questions Answered in FAQ

1. *Does a ministry that addresses the work of evil spirits bring particular danger?*

2. *The Bible says the enemy is like a roaring lion, seeking to devour us. What about spiritual attacks and retaliation against my family and me because of my ministry?*

3. *What do I do if, after listening to a story of terrible abuse and evil, I go away feeling oppressed or slimed?*

4. *What advice would you give to someone who feels called to this ministry but struggles with fear?*

5. *How do I know if someone has been cursed?*

6. *I have heard you say we should know our strengths and weaknesses—we should know our own soul. Why is introspection a problem?*

7. *Do I lead people to forgive God?*

8. *How do I handle generational healing and generational spirits?*

9. *Can I use the Five Keys to pray with children?*

10. *I have heard you say not to dig during a session, but I have noticed you ask many questions. Can you clarify?*

11. *How do I screen people who request ministry?*

12. *How do I know if someone has a serious mental illness? Should I minister to him or her?*

13. *Are there limits to confidentiality?*

14. *Why do you not speak the "blood of Jesus" in your battle with demons?*

15. *Why don't you teach people to bind the spirits when praying for someone to be liberated?*

16. *If Jesus has already bound the spirits and we exercise our faith according to that truth, then how should we understand "binding" in Matthew 16:19 and Matthew 18:19?*

17. *Why don't you teach people to pray a cleansing prayer after ministry?*

18. *I do not think I will be comfortable praying for deliverance without using a cleansing and a binding prayer. Does this mean I cannot participate in* UNBOUND *ministry teams?*

19. *I have years of experience in confrontational deliverance. Help me make the transition to the* UNBOUND *model.*

20. *I am a trained counselor. Is there a way for me to use* UNBOUND *in my practice?*

21. *Do you always pray in the name of Jesus? What if I am ministering to a Hindu or a Muslim or a Jew?*

CHAPTER 10
Growing in Leadership

QUESTION #1
Does a ministry that addresses the work of evil spirits bring particular danger?

ANSWER

There is a lot of fear associated with deliverance ministry. UNBOUND ministry shifts the focus from demons to the person. This approach will help you leave behind any fear of evil spirits. The answer is no. You should not experience any greater level of spiritual attacks and temptations than you have doing other forms of service like leading evangelistic outreaches or going on missions. I (Neal) would have to say there was a much greater spiritual battle over the years in parenting my four sons.

FURTHER REFLECTION

Once, while praying for a man with my hand holding his arm, I felt evil creep up my arm. Because I knew the enemy could not enter me unless there was an entryway, I had no fear or concern and I was not distracted from what I was doing, which was to help the person find freedom. Another time—and this is very rare—a demon said aloud, "Do you think you are going to get away with this?" The utter conviction with which the threat was spoken made me laugh since it is contrary to what I know to be true. "Nothing will harm you," Jesus says in Luke 10 (verse 19 NIV).

In any case, most of the attacks and temptations that come to me tend to rise up out of my own areas of weakness. I have come home from ministry trips discouraged by relationship conflicts and quite exhausted. After a few days, I realize there is more to the exhaustion than jetlag or lack of sleep. When I ask Janet to pray with me by taking me through some of the keys and helping me to name my enemies, I am able to shake off the oppression. My enemies are old enemies I can recognize quickly. They like to target areas of personal weakness.

One UNBOUND leader expressed the attack on her areas of weakness like this:

> One particular "attack" I often experience before praying with people is a strong sense of inadequacy—I have nothing to offer. But I also see this not as an attack, but a reality check that God allows me to have. I don't have anything to offer. Another "attack" I experience is pride: I'm so good at this; I'm a natural. This is my temptation—Satan sees vulnerability, yes, but more important, he's desperately trying to remove me from the source of real grace and power. So, you see, it is my own "junk" that troubles me when I minister. I just treat this as the normal spiritual warfare that we all encounter—after all, there's a lot of other stuff in my life that can stir the pot and make me vulnerable besides ministry.

There is one other reason why you may experience what feels like an upswing in spiritual warfare: God is asking you to take new territory. You should expect a battle when you are taking new territory for the kingdom. New challenges can also bring spiritual resistance that is related to natural anxieties and a tendency to doubt. Again, the Lord wants to continue to deliver you from these doubts and fears. He has promised to give you the land—so be like the Israelites at Jericho, confident that God is with you and will give you victory. When you move through a time of resistance into a time of peace, you will know your enemies have been defeated and you are walking in a new level of authority for service in the kingdom.

Jesus is, of course, your true model. He was tempted and certainly had trials, but He never got mad at the devil; He never blamed the devil for His trials or focused on the enemy. He focused solely on the

Father's will and either ignored the enemy (remained asleep in the boat), resisted the enemy's temptation (quoted Scriptures), or rebuked the enemy (in the desert and in Peter) as He yielded to the will of God. He daily poured out His heart to His Father, and as He proclaimed the kingdom, He advanced it by driving out spirits. Scriptures even interpret Jesus' passion and death as the will of the Father rather than as retaliation from the enemy. Jesus obediently took on the sins of the world and experienced in His humanity the full weight of the evil that entered us through sin. Your attitudes are to be the same as His.

Question #2

But the Bible says the enemy is like a roaring lion, seeking to devour us. What about spiritual attacks and retaliation against my family and me because of my ministry?

Answer

Spiritual warfare is a normal part of the Christian life. It is part of living in the kingdom here on earth. Spiritual attacks include everything from temptation, to the daily trials of living in a fallen world, to a more intense season of attack on your identity and well-being. The benefit of Unbound is that it can help you overcome spiritual attacks in every situation. But you should *not* expect retaliation (or what some call "kickback") from the enemy when you step out in ministry, for you are under the Lord's protection. And it would be a mistake to give the devil attention by interpreting trials and temptation as retaliation. The enemy cannot do anything to you that God does not permit for your ultimate good.

Further Reflection

Many leaders in deliverance ministry and those who do exorcisms have said they experienced retaliation. They tell stories about oppression coming on them, visitation by demonic presences, and torment or temptation that is intensified by an evil spiritual presence. Often, they share this to warn us that such retaliation might occur and that praying for deliverance can be dangerous. This becomes a clarion call for the necessity of intense prayer for protection.

If by *retaliation* you mean "to return like for like; pay back injury for injury," then no, you should not experience retaliation when you follow the UNBOUND model. Nothing can separate you from the love of God in Christ Jesus, so do not expect evil to return onto your own head. Those of us who minister using UNBOUND do not confront, battle, or provoke demons. As such, we have no expectation of unusual demonic attacks and it does not happen. I do not doubt the stories of others and I know there are many mysteries I do not understand and cannot explain. I can only answer the question from our experience within the context of UNBOUND ministry and the faith we have been given. We are aware that stories and warnings of retaliation may linger in the minds of those we train, however. This itself can be the basis for fear or unbelief and can open the door to the enemy (see *Resisting the Devil*, Appendix B).

Because I get the question about retaliation so often, I passed it on to some UNBOUND leaders in different cities for further clarification. Here are two of the responses I received:

> I don't think about retaliation from the enemy while preparing or while praying the UNBOUND model with someone. My focus is on the person I am praying with and on Jesus. I prepare by praying to be in tune to the Holy Spirit, by praying that I don't get in the way of our Lord, and by praying that I may hear Him and love the person with all of my heart. I try to prepare my heart also by praying against pride, perhaps skipping a meal, or going to confession. You say that deliverance is about freedom and freedom is all about Jesus, not the enemy. I guess I have received that message.
>
> The Africans I prayed with in Ghana have had more obvious interaction with evil spirits in their lives than we are used to here in North America. Yet there were no evil effects, nor signs of the enemy gaining any power or bothering any one of us on the team while ministering to them. We ministered to many people in Ghana and heard many stories of fetish priests, libations offered [to spirits], curses that were passed from generation to generation, visits to the spirits for good luck, and [syncretism], yet the simple, effective five-key model had the same results there as in our country. We all walked away free in Christ!

One of the leaders did mention an increase in normal spiritual warfare. She said:

> In the two years that I have used the UNBOUND model, I have prayed for many people, including some tough cases—such as folks who had had heavy-duty occult involvement. On occasion, I have experienced very strong temptations one or two days before praying, but I have prayed through the keys [of UNBOUND] and it has taken care of that problem. It seems that the temptation to fight or argue and the temptation to sin in general increases before I minister with UNBOUND, but without exception, once I have followed the Five Keys in prayer, there is always very good fruit: I have abundant freedom and no doubts that I am protected by our Lord when I go and pray.

All Christians experience the times of increased temptation she mentions. This is expected spiritual warfare. In Ephesians 6, we are warned not to think about our struggles only in light of what we see. The bigger, unseen reality behind our struggles against our fallen nature and against the natural pressures from the world around us is that we have an enemy who uses all sorts of tactics—subtle and not-so-subtle—to undermine our faith. But not all trials come from the enemy.

Sometimes what feels to us like an attack of the enemy is really testing from God. In Deuteronomy 8, Moses reminds the Israelites that "the LORD your God has led you these forty years in the wilderness, that He might humble you, testing you to know what was in your heart, whether you would keep His commandments, or not." You have been set free; you have had your Exodus, but perhaps you are tempted to return to trusting in your own strength. God's desire is to expose any subtle return to idolatry, and He will often expose your idolatry by allowing an attack at a point of weakness that is particular to you. Other times, though, He just wants to take you deeper, expose the next layer, and build your faith higher. It is good to examine yourself when your heart is troubled and make sure you have not placed your hopes or your expectations on yourself in any way but only on God. It is good to seek more deliverance and healing. None of us is ever finished with our journey through repentance toward rest as long as we live on earth.

Question #3

What do I do if, after listening to a story of terrible abuse and evil, I go away feeling oppressed or slimed?

Answer

Evil presents itself in the form of thoughts and images. If you receive those thoughts and images and do not filter them through your faith in the Lord Jesus, you may be opening the doors to oppression. We suggest you use Luke 10:17 as your model. The disciples "returned with joy, saying, 'Lord, even the demons are subject to us in Your name!'" As you rejoice and give thanks to God for what He has done during the session, you are washed clean of evil.

Further Reflection

It may also help to think about what Scripture says about childbirth: "A woman giving birth to a child has pain because her time has come; but when her baby is born she forgets the anguish because of her joy that a child is born into the world" (John 16:21 NIV). Typically, your team will "forget" the evil as you celebrate the grace of redemption at work in a person's life. If the joy of the Lord is not present with the final prayers of thanksgiving and blessing, the team leader should ask each member of the team how they are doing following the session. If there is a need, pray with one another, quickly using any of the Five Keys that might be helpful. Among those with training and experience this is rarely necessary, for each team member has been personally equipped with the Five Keys and a basic understanding of the power of the Scriptures: "Submit yourselves, therefore, to God. Resist the devil, and he will flee from you" (James 4:7). But you should not hesitate to pray with one another whenever a doubt or fear has taken a grip on a team member.

If a team member feels "slimed," view this as an opportunity for growth in freedom and maturity, not for fear. Consider three possible entryways that may need to be dealt with:

1. *If you have taken in an image of evil out of curiosity or found yourself attracted to the evil and allowed your thoughts to dwell on it apart from faith, you do need to be cleansed.* (Key #1—repentance and faith are important here). As you listened to the story, of course you wanted to find out what happened and how the person responded. But you did not need the gory details. You needed only enough to help them be truthful and honest in their response to the Lord. If you pressed for details, repent of salacious curiosity.

2. *Sometimes you listen to a story that is very like your own.* If you have wounds that have not yet been fully healed, hearing the story from another's mouth may bring feelings of oppression. If you can recognize this as an opportunity for deeper freedom, you will not interpret your experience as a general oppression.

3. *Consider the possibility of pride.* A priest called me after several months of using the UNBOUND model to help people. He felt oppressed. I reviewed with him several possibilities that may have opened the door to his oppression. He immediately knew what it was. It was pride. He could pinpoint the time on the weekend retreat that pride came through in his preaching following a powerful ministry session. He repented, was prayed for, and the oppression left. After learning this lesson, he has not had any repetition of this oppression over the years as he has continued to pray for the captives to be set free. Pride and any sin that is an expression of pride—like unrighteous judgment, criticism, comparison, and the like—may be an entryway for the enemy. If you approach ministry with an air of self-confidence, self-reliance, and superiority, God Himself may allow the enemy to attack you for your ultimate good. "God opposes the proud but gives grace to the humble" (1 Peter 5:5b).

No matter what the reason, be thankful you have an opportunity for growth. Dealing with the entryway is much more fruitful than repeatedly dealing with the symptom.

QUESTION #4

What advice would you give to someone who feels called to this ministry but struggles with fear?

ANSWER

Applying the Five Keys, which are based on fundamental truths, will help you escape the grip of fear and walk in freedom. Remember that the enemy cannot oppress a believer unless he first finds a place of agreement within them. The serpent did not invade or force Adam and Eve to sin. He seduced them with his lies, tempting them to sin. The pattern is the same today. Fear is always an expression of unbelief and mistrust.

The most powerful antidote to fear of the devil and his power is to know the love of God and to know the promises that flow out of His character. Expose all fears to the light of His love and ask Him to renew your mind and heal your heart so you can trust in His love. Then you will be better able to carry your faith into the realm of ministry and take your stand on God's truth.

Remember: deliverance ministry is a ministry of love. His love!

FURTHER REFLECTION

Our belief system is the foundation for our practice. If you believe the truth—the revelation of God's love in Jesus Christ—you need not fear the devil or his works. You have what you need to overcome your fears. What truths do you need to stand upon?

1. *God is a good Father.* Hebrews 12:7 says "Endure hardship as discipline; God is treating you as sons. For what son is not disciplined by his father" (NIV). God allows the enemy to test you for your benefit. The trials that He sends reveal areas of sin, bondage, deception, and vulnerability that you can renounce and from which you will gain greater freedom if you allow the suffering to do its work. Testing should never deter you from trusting in God's love for you.

    Believe also the truth of Romans 8:28: "And we know that in all things God works for the good of those who love Him, who have been called according to His purpose" (NIV). Also, practice giving thanks for the work that every trial will do in your life. "Give thanks in all circumstances; for this is the will of God in Christ Jesus for you" (1 Thessalonians 5:18).

2. *You will never be tested beyond the grace God gives you to endure.* The apostle Paul is clear: "No temptation has overtaken you that is not common to man. God is faithful, and He will not let you be tempted beyond your strength, but with the temptation will also provide the way of escape, that you may be able to endure it" (1 Cor. 10:13).

3. *Nothing will harm you.* In Luke 10:19, Jesus says to His disciples, "I have given you authority to trample on snakes and scorpions and to overcome all the power of the enemy; nothing will harm you" (NIV). This promise came as Jesus sent out His disciples to heal the sick and proclaim the kingdom of God. With the proclamation, demons were driven out. The disciples returned with joy, saying, "Even the demons submit to us in Your name."

   If you are sent, if you are doing the works of Jesus and are proclaiming the kingdom, then indeed this promise belongs to you as well. Remember that nothing means *nothing*.

4. *Remember: Perfect love casts out fear* (1 John 4:18). Keeping these basic principles in mind will keep you from being impressed with the devil and will help you interpret your experiences according to the truth.

CHAPTER 11

Ministry Issues

QUESTION #5

How do I know if someone has been cursed?

ANSWER

You do not know unless God tells you. There may be signs of ongoing tragedy and demonic attacks that may make you suspicious, but you do not know. Usually when people ask this question, they are fearful of what seems to be a mysterious attack of the enemy; something seems to come from a source outside of them and makes them feel helpless. This is just where the enemy wants them, doubting that they have power in Jesus to do anything about their situation. The devil always wants them to think they are under his power—under a curse.

FURTHER REFLECTION

In the UNBOUND model, we do not try to discern the precise external source of trouble or focus too heavily on what the person presents as the source of their spiritual problem. Even if someone gets a revelation of what it is (a word of knowledge), listen to the whole story and help him respond at every level. Use each key, regardless of what the person thinks is the primary cause of their problem. Ask them about any occult involvement they or their family members may have dabbled in. Ask if there are any occult objects present in the home. Address all these issues in ministry, but be aware that the intensity of spiritual warfare—which appears to come from one source—may be obscuring a more foundational issue that holds the key to freedom (e.g., surrender to the Lord, forgiveness of Mom and Dad, or renouncing the fear of being cursed).

The individual may be under unbelief, which keeps him from believing in and taking hold of the victory already given him in Christ. If someone is experiencing oppression or obsession, it is always an opportunity for them to discover more deeply the height and breadth and depth of God's love and to surrender more fully to the Lord and receive His mercy and love. Jesus is our model. He did not take His direction from the devil or seek information from him. His heart was singularly focused on the Father, saying and doing what He saw the Father saying and doing.

A good question to ask the person is, "Who told you that you were cursed?" Follow that with questions such as "What is God saying to you?" Find out if they honestly seek to know Jesus' voice. Listen carefully in the Spirit to discern what lies have kept them from the faith to hear from God and to trust His voice, or what fear overrides their faith. If sin has not been confessed or past agreement with the lies of the enemy has not been named and renounced in the "name of Jesus," a door has been left open to other visitors that may come by means of a curse. It is just as important to understand the door the individual opened which allowed them to receive the curse as it is to understand the curse itself. I believe if you deal with the doorway, then the source will also become known if necessary.

If a person lacks understanding of how an evil spirit gains influence, the evil they face will often appear like a mystery. A curse is a reasonable explanation for the unknown source of evil, but if they believe they are cursed and unable to help themselves or get help from others, they will be in a very difficult and rather hopeless place. If well-meaning Christians have reinforced that idea, the fear can grow and, with it, the power of the evil. Never discount someone's belief that they were cursed. Instead, help them to understand the truth that an evil spirit needs a familiar place to rest.

Proverbs 26:2 says, "Like a fluttering sparrow or a darting swallow, an undeserved curse does not come to rest" (NIV). It would be a mistake to interpret this proverb as a reason for guilt. "I am cursed because I deserve it." If they have sinned and brought evil on themselves, they can repent and receive forgiveness. They can know, as they actively love God, that evil that has touched their life will be turned to good. In the Gospel of John we read, "But to all who received Him, who believed in His name, He gave power to become children of God" (John 1:12). If the person has received the Savior and believes Jesus is Lord, they have power now to exercise the authority they have as God's son or daughter. They can take their stand against the schemes of the enemy.

But they must be taught. Every Christian needs to be taught how to receive the power to live as child of God. So work to help them recognize their responsibility and the power they have. I have found that most curses are received because of unbelief (or faith in the lie). If a person responds in fear to the words or actions of others or if they believe what was said, they open the door to the power of the words spoken against them. Superstition or a superficial understanding of the Christian faith makes them vulnerable to receiving the curse. Spend time evangelizing and teaching people's minds and hearts on the truth of the gospel.

QUESTION #6

I have heard you say we should know our strengths and weaknesses—we should know our own soul. Why is introspection a problem?

ANSWER

Let me quote what I said in *UNBOUND* to answer that question: "Introspection…is self-focused—a desire to help oneself. It places me, rather than Jesus Christ, at the center" (p.124). Prayerful reflection is a healthy practice in our spiritual life. But introspection is unaided self-thought. It is the opposite of insights given by the Holy Spirit. Our fallen minds are turned on our selves, our needs, our problems and we get further and further into the mire of self-analysis. Properly listening to the Holy Spirit frees us from "the hell of introspection" as Leanne Payne puts it. The problem with introspection is that of all the exercises of the intellect, it is the one most caught in a continuous spiral inward. It assumes there is no standard outside the self.

Further Reflection

Can there ever be healthy introspection? I do not think so. This may be confusing because some ministries use the inner look as an important part of healing. It can certainly be fruitful to examine our own feelings, thoughts, and motives, even in a detailed manner. At times, our patterns of thought, motives, and behavior need to be prayerfully examined. If done within a healthy relationship with God, self, and others, this examination is a healthy scrutiny of our conscience in preparation for ministry, for confession, or for the Lord's Supper. But this is not introspection. We would more accurately call it self-examination, consideration, contemplation, or reflection.

Introspection is the fallen mind looking at the fallen self. It ignores God as the source of truth, and thus can open the door to all sorts of lies of the enemy. Self-condemnation, guilt, blame, hopelessness, self-hatred, despair, and even suicidal thoughts may quickly rush in where introspection reigns. Bill Johnson, in *When Heaven Invades Earth*, expresses the danger of unhealthy introspection:

> I struggled for many years with self-evaluation. The main problem was that I never found anything good in me. It always led to discouragement, which led to doubt, and eventually took me to unbelief. Somehow, I had developed the notion that this was how I could become holy—by showing tremendous concern for my own motives.
>
> It may sound strange, but I don't examine my motives anymore. That's not my job. I work hard to obey God in everything that I am and do. ... After many years of trying to do what only He could do, I discovered I was not the Holy Spirit. I cannot convict and deliver myself of sin. Does that mean I never deal with impure motives? No. He has shown Himself to be very eager to point out my constant need for repentance and change. But He's the one with the spotlight and He alone can give the grace to change.
>
> There is a major difference between the believer who is being dealt with by God and the one who has become introspective.

> When God searches the heart, He finds things in us that He wants to change. He brings conviction because of His commitment to deliver us. ...I do not do well when I look inward... (pp. 147-48)

This is my story as well. I do not do well when I look inward. There is plenty right before me to deal with. I find that relationships, in particular marriage, are God's provision for helping me see my sin. When sinful actions and attitudes are exposed, I am most ready to deal with the deep roots of my sin. Then I am most ready to reflect on what is going on inside. My reflection cannot start or end with introspection, however. If I get stuck in some pattern of thinking where I am only seeing a black cloud, I find someone to talk to and try to express what is going on inside. The Holy Spirit brings conviction, not condemnation. My purpose is not to understand the black cloud but to gain victory over it and move back to doing what God wants me to do in the way He wants me to do it.

In her UNBOUND talk, "Staying Free: the Battle for the Mind," Ann Stevens makes a very helpful distinction between introspection and reflection:

> We really need to learn to become reflective people—not introspective, but reflective—and learn to lead reflective lives. Introspection is digging around inside trying to come up with something; being reflective is being aware of what has already risen to the surface. We need to become aware of what is actually going on in our mind, our thought processes, our thought patterns... Satan loves unreflective souls because he can just set up his schemes, his strongholds of lies and wrong thinking, and sit back and watch us wonder why we can't seem to get it right.
>
> ...Introspection is working too hard, over-analyzing, trying to "figure it out." Reflection is realizing, for example, "Oh, this thought always comes to mind when I'm angry!" It is recognizing what is already going on, listening to the tape recorder that goes off in our heads when we are provoked or under stress.

Question #7
Do I lead people to forgive God?

Answer

Theologically, forgiving God does not make much sense. God has never sinned, nor has He ever done anything wrong towards us. In that sense, how can anyone "forgive God"?

But this is not to say that there are not real emotions to recognize in people who come to us for help. They do blame God, feel betrayed by Him, let down by Him, feel unprotected by Him, etc. But this truly is not because God has done anything wrong. It is because we have falsely interpreted things in such a way that "God is to blame." This then leads people into bondage. At the root is a fundamental lack of recognition of the truth. There is a confusion as to who God is, a failure to embrace the fact that God truly is love. Our wounds, misjudgments and accusations prevent us from seeing the real love of God.

What needs to happen in these situations is to lead the person to freedom by helping them to grieve and see the truth of who God is, and repent of any false ways they have seen or understood God. When people blame Him, accuse Him, and judge Him, there is a fundamental lack of recognition of the truth of who He is and who they are. We do not want to reinforce this. Instead, lead people to freedom through repentance without reinforcing unbelief.

Further reflection

All of us suffer loss and experience the evils that entered our world through sin. In order to grow toward Christian maturity, we have to learn how to process these losses and disappointments. The same is true for the one who comes to you for prayer. Whether spoken or not, they may have held expectations that God would intervene to save them, prevent a tragedy, or preserve their children from the enemy's plans. They may have been filled with hope for their marriage, holding to what they believed to be God's promises for a future of happiness and fruitfulness, only to find themselves confused and distant from God because of deep disappointment. Or they may have prayed for years for a healing but have yet to see it. In each case, disappointment with God has placed limits on the freedom to trust Him.

The fact that God did not show up the way they expected Him to does not mean He did anything wrong. God's every action is motivated by divine love. He never acts outside of our best interests, even though we may *feel* or *believe* He has not been good to us. While these feelings are very real, they are not based on truth.

Some have suggested it may be practically helpful during an UNBOUND prayer session to have the person say, "I forgive God." But this would not be dealing in truth or reality. The person needs to know that their feeling of betrayal is real; but they also need to work through this, seeing that whatever happened to them has led them to not trust God. They need to express grief over the situation, but then they also need to see that God has not wounded them, but surrounds even this area with His love. We cannot always understand this with our minds, but we can know that God is always loving and trustworthy.

Part of the healing here is helping the person to repent of their judgment of God and turn to Him in trust. As we help someone express their pain and lead them in repentance, they will be further equipped to have honest conversations with God as they go through the tragedies and disappointments of life. Expressing forgiveness toward God is not part of the UNBOUND model.

When we lead someone to forgive another person (e.g., a parent), we are not in a position to judge whether the parents were wrong or righteous in their behavior. Our focus is on their story and on the person's experience as mediated through their feelings. And whatever the truth of the situation, if they feel a wound from another, forgiveness needs to be given. As we lead them to forgive, we help them process their experience through the power Christ has given them to forgive. When someone is upset at God, however, we know this anger is directed at eternal righteousness. What should they do with their anger?

I have learned it is most helpful to have them express their pain and anger to God. They can do this by saying they do not understand why God did or did not do some particular thing. If they expected God to act in a different way, they have permission to tell Him they felt abandoned, forsaken, or overlooked—or whatever reaction they had to what they perceived as inaction on God's part. Once they have expressed these feelings, it is appropriate to lead them to humble themselves before the Lord and ask forgiveness for judging Him, accusing Him, or thinking they loved their sick child more than He does. After this, have them tell the Lord, "I do trust You," or "I want to trust You again"; have them ask for His help; and, by faith, have them surrender to the will of God, who loves them.

Helping others to deal with grief is necessary work. People often bury their feelings, either because they know they are not supposed to be mad at God, or because they would just rather not face what is below the surface. If listening and helping others is not part of normal church life, unresolved grief may remain hidden until there is a special moment of grace or a crisis that brings an individual to their knees, ready to do whatever it takes.

I once prayed with a very competent Christian leader as part of the training for a conference. Though there was nothing really urgent or obvious to be dealt with, I still needed to lead her though the keys so others could learn. A bit of conversation did not reveal anything except a recent disappointment, and I found myself writing down "disappointment" and circling it. It was all I had. But we kept talking. When I thought she felt safe with me, I asked, "Were there any other big disappointments earlier in your life?" Wham! Bam! The Holy Spirit began to move and her eyes filled up. With a bit of anger in her voice, she said she had dealt with it and did not want to talk about it again. Then, with a very small amount of encouragement, she went on to tell me of her first love. At fourteen, she gave her heart and body to a boy she was convinced she would be with for the rest of her life. She was lied to and betrayed by him. Without this opportunity for ministry, her grief at this very great betrayal might have stayed hidden for many more years. She needed freedom. It was not about the sin, for that was long ago repented of, but about the deep pain and grief that kept her from freedom in her relationship with the Lord and her husband.

While UNBOUND MINISTRY is not focused on doing "grief work," we regularly help people resolve their unresolved grief. Theresa Burke, PhD., my friend who founded Rachel's Vineyard, writes:

Working through grief requires confronting one's loss, admitting the loss, grieving the loss, learning to live with the loss and working through the grief to find a renewed sense of meaning or purpose beyond the loss. Each of these processes must be successfully completed in order to resolve one's grief. This is what therapists call "grief work." It is called "work" because it can be a laborious process that takes time and effort.[1]

She also writes, "Grief is more than a single emotion. It can include feelings of loss, confusion, loneliness, anger, despair and more. Grief can be overpowering. It can penetrate and darken every corner of one's life."

And that is the point. Unresolved grief is a huge doorway through which the enemy loves to run. Unresolved grief leads to resentment toward God that can be carried for a long time. If someone is aware of their resentment toward God, they will be able to point you to the source. But you need to look beyond the source. How have the tentacles of their response to disappointment or loss affected how they experience life? Sadness may be rooted in deep loss that has never been allowed to surface. Anger directed at themselves or others may be a means of avoidance of their deeper anger with God. It takes faith to be angry with God; it requires truth to be set free. Burke writes about this, calling it "disenfranchised grief." She says:

> When a person experiences secret sorrow that cannot be shared or confronted, this is called "disenfranchised grief." The term "disenfranchised" means to be denied the freedom or license to do something. In this case, it means being denied permission to openly display one's grief. This makes it far more difficult to complete the grief process, and may not only prolong one's grief but also make it worse. Such "impacted" grief can even become integrated into one's personality and touch every aspect of one's life.[2]

---

[1] Theresa Burke, Ph.D., and David C. Reardon, *Forbidden Grief: The Unspoken Pain of Abortion* (Springfield, IL: Acorn Books, 2002), 48.

[2] Ibid., 49.

So do you lead people to forgive God for the pain He caused? No, He did not cause it. But we do help them get in touch with the pain in their lives and bring it before the Lord in truth. We listen to them until the grief has had a chance to be expressed, before leading the believer to repent of their unrighteous judgments of God that developed in response to their loss. We assist them in renouncing spirits and negative emotions of anger, resentment, bitterness, unforgiveness... As we gently bring them through this process, we keep in mind the mission of Jesus: to bring the person to reconciliation with the Father through the Son.

QUESTION #8
How do you handle generational healing and generational spirits?

ANSWER
Though the UNBOUND model does not speak specifically of generational healing, praying through family patterns and sins is part of what we do as we focus on helping each person take responsibility and, through the name of Jesus, end the oppression in their own generation.

FURTHER REFLECTION
A few simple examples may help. Kim, who did not bond with her mother, suffers a host of issues she needs help with. The interview might go something like this:

"How did your mom get along with her mom?"

"They were not very close."

"Is there anything about your grandmother that was unusual?"

"She was an orphan."

"Do you ever feel like an orphan?"

"Yes, I do."

From there you might inquire about related spirits such as those of homelessness, loss, fatherlessness, motherlessness, rejection, and abandonment. Kim's acknowledgement that she feels like an orphan gives great insight into why she has such trouble bonding with her own children. As you help her see the connection to the tragedy in her grandmother's life, she will be able to identify areas where she is under spiritual bondage.

If Jack says he has no problem no problem with anger and rage but shares that his father had a lot of rage and violent behavior, you might ask about his grandparents. If he says, as he very well might, his dad's father was a violent alcoholic, you now have more direction about him and what spirits he might be in bondage to. Jack grew up under generational rage and violence but did not yield to it. Did he overcome the generational pattern by the grace of God or did he choose the different path out of fear, insecurity, and rejection? Did he make a vow to never become like his dad or to never be angry? It is important to talk here about resentment and bitterness, for they form a low-level foundation for the cluster of anger, rage, revenge, violence, and hatred—and the spirit of murder. Now is also the time to find out more about family patterns. How did Jack's own father respond to *his* father? How did Jack respond to Jack's father? What structures were present in the family and what structures of thinking did Jack build because of the verbal abuse he suffered?

Dan struggles with a poor self-image. He is plagued by shame, fear of embarrassment, and guilt, and he does not know why. You might ask Dan if there was anything unusual in his family history.

"No one ever talked about my great uncle. I only found out I had an uncle by accident. I think he was in prison and may have murdered someone."

Often in an UNBOUND session, people bring up things they have never talked about. They have learned to live with the darkness of uncertainty, anticipating a rebuke or denial if they ask about the event. An event like this is much bigger than praying for the uncle or even renouncing a spirit of murder. Whatever the tragic event was, the road the family was on took a turn and it affected everyone. Since the situation was kept secret and was not brought into the light of God's Word and His presence, the enemy has a place to rest. Dan does not need to go back to his family to find out what happened in order to be healed. He does need you to help him take hold of the freedom he has in Christ so he will not walk in the path his family chose: living in denial by burying the shame of the past. When he experiences freedom, perhaps he can help others in his family choose truth and light, deal with the historical reality, and overcome fear and shame.

Knowing what the "black sheep" did is not as important as exposing patterns of thought and behavior that reflect a family's reactions to the "black sheep." Shame; secrecy; a fear that something's wrong with the individual or the family; and perhaps even bondage to hiding, escape, lying, and denial can all develop or deepen in a family system traumatized by one member's actions.

Occult practice in a family tree may bring great destruction on the present generation. If you discover older generations practiced any form of the occult, lead the individual to renounce the spirit that operated in _____ and any spirit that came to them through_____. Have them break the power of any words or claim made upon their life. If bondage comes through their parents, have them say, "I break any unholy tie with my mom/dad and I renounce the spirit that was at work in her/him." Sometimes a child is designated by the family member operating under a spirit as the one who will carry the "gift." This claim must be renounced and the power of it broken.

It is good to be aware of patterns of spiritual weakness in the family tree, for it puts the believer in touch with deeply personal and familiar patterns of thought and behaviors. Knowing these patterns gives insight and can uncover both the good and the bad hidden within. It is also important for each believer to honor their mother, father, and all those who have gone before them, and thank God for the sacrifice and spiritual heritage they have received. Make sure that in rejecting a broken family pattern or behavior, the individual does not also reject their parents. To reject one's parents is to reject a part of oneself and close off part of one's personality that needs to be expressed and sanctified by the action of the Holy Spirit. Another danger I have seen is the tendency to look at the sins of the ancestors and subtly shift responsibility for one's sin and weakness to the sins of the others. Each believer is responsible for their own choices even if their free will was severely limited by what happened to them. They have received a heritage for good and bad and now they have a responsibility to cooperate with the grace of God, bringing them to redemption.

When the individual was baptized into Christ, they were "born of water and the Spirit" (John 3:5). Because of this, they truly are a new creation. But if there is no renewal of their mind, an internal structure of thinking and believing that is consistent with darkness and in agreement with it remains. Evil spirits will be able to quickly reassert themselves. If the atmosphere in the home as they grew up was not free from various expressions of darkness, an evil spirit that is familiar to the family's way of thinking and acting can still affect them. Because they have grown accustomed to its presence, the spirit has been able to send down deep roots.[3] Generational healing comes when they are able to recognize and renounce these patterns in their own life. Their freedom will remain as they are transformed by the renewal of their mind (Romans 12:1). In Appendix A, you will find a testimony of the healing of at least three generations of a spirit of fear. Both a mother and a daughter are walking in new freedom, freedom for which they must continue to fight as they walk by the Spirit. "It is for freedom that Christ has set us free. Stand firm, then, and do not let yourselves be burdened again by a yoke of slavery… So I say, live by the Spirit, and you will not gratify the desires of the sinful nature." (Galatians 5:1, 16 NIV).

QUESTION #9

Can I use the Five Keys to pray with children?[4]

ANSWER

Yes! We know that when we break with our enemies and take hold of freedom in Christ, we are gaining an inheritance for the generations that follow us. Therefore, it is always best to start by ministering to the parents. When parents uncover hidden lies they have believed and break the power of their influence in their own lives, they also become aware of influences and deceptions to which their children are vulnerable.

---

[3] For a deeper understanding of how spirits work, see the appendix of *Resisting the Devil*.

[4] In a church or other "official" capacity such as at a retreat, conference, or ongoing ministry, you will need to first learn about local/national laws concerning how to handle certain incidents a minor might reveal to you in the course of prayer, such as being molested. Your church/parish may also have additional moral guidelines or requirements such as courses you will need to take, background checks, etc.

As they receive and understand the simplicity of the Five Keys, they are equipped to assist their children.

Further reflection

When I am asked to pray with children, I know a child's issue is a family issue and if I am to say yes, I need the parents to make a commitment to receive personal ministry as well. If you are asked to pray for a child but find the parents are not open to ministry for themselves, I recommend you proceed with caution in using the Five Keys.

Ideally, you will pray for the parents and teach them how to minister to their children. If a parent is set free from spiritual bondage that is also afflicting their child, they have great authority over the enemies that have been named and defeated. If the child is very young, the parent may find it effective to pray over them as they sleep. As the parent names the enemies from which they have been set free and commands them to leave, their child can be set free—now that the spiritual atmosphere has changed. Parents who have been set free themselves and who are learning to walk in their own freedom can easily lead a cooperative child with simple, everyday fears to freedom by using the Five Keys. But what if there is a serious disorder in the child? The help the child and family needs may require a variety of forms of assistance, but that does not mean we should not expect the child to be helped by a solid understanding and simple application of the Five Keys.

If the parents do not feel they can minister to the child alone, the second best approach is to have them present as you pray with the child. You will have a window into the family dynamic through seeing the child with their parents. This is not always possible. Not every child will feel safe or open with parents present.

Praying with a post-pubescent child is a different story. As a child grows, they must leave behind the faith of a child, which is dependent on their parents, and take up their responsibility to choose Jesus as their own Lord and Savior. Their choice to follow the Lord for themselves forms the solid basis for any sustained freedom. During adolescence, they enter into an even deeper battle for the will; the choice to surrender to God and seek freedom must now be theirs. This choice must be made repeatedly in correspondence to their growing development as a person. If the teen is willing to seek help, you will find the Five Keys of UNBOUND may be very helpful in evangelizing them and helping them identify the lies of the enemy.

In either case, I strongly recommend you have experience successfully using the Five Keys *before* you pray for someone else's child and that those who are overseeing your ministry approve.

Let me share the story of one mother's success in praying with her child:

> This morning I had a blessed moment of UNBOUND prayer with my four-year-old daughter who, with tears, brought up an old issue. I knew we had to pray. Though only four, she followed me in prayer with no problem because we had done it a few times before. After the command, I asked, "How do you feel?"
>
> "I feel good," she said.
>
> When I blessed her, I could literally see her teary eyes turn into eyes full of joy. I did not need to ask again, but I did.
>
> "How do you feel?"
>
> "I feel great!" She started running around and around, yelling, "Weehee, yeehah!" and giggling.
>
> After about ten minutes of this, I said, "You are happy, huh?!"
>
> "Yes, Mama. I am happy. I am very happy!"
>
> The change [in my daughter] was 360 degrees! I thank God for the gift He has given us through you!

I followed up and found out this was the fourth time in a year this mother had helped her daughter using the Five Keys. One time she guided her four-year-old to forgive a bully for pushing her down at the park. She said, "It was as if the poison from a thorn was removed from her daughter's spirit."

ONE MOTHER'S ADVICE

Keep the prayer short—around five minutes. I just pray and ask the Holy Spirit to show me where my daughter might be stuck, and then I ask her simple short questions: Are you sad? Do you want to get rid of that sadness? Are you feeling angry? How angry? With whom?

Why? Are you happy when you are feeling angry? Of course she says No, mama," so then I ask, "Do you want to get rid of that anger?"

She nods. "Yes."

I take her through repentance: "Jesus, I am sorry I got angry…" "In the name of Jesus, I forgive… for…." Then "I lead her to renounce the spirit of sadness, anger, and so on. I tell my daughter to close her eyes and stay quiet and she does—she really does! I say the word of command and ask her how she feels. She always has had a great answer. We say thanks and then I bless her. It can be very quick, but always so very powerful."

This mother taught her daughter that to *renounce* means to "kick out," and when she takes authority she says, "By the authority given to me as Isabelle's mother and as a Christian, I command any evil spirit to leave now in the name of Jesus."[5]

Another mom and dad reported an even briefer prayer:

Our five-year-old son was deathly afraid of storms and we finally figured out that he had watched a television news program about dangerous storms that killed people. We led him to renounce the fear that entered when he watched the program and I commanded the fear to leave. He has shown no signs of that fear since!

Equipping Our Children for Life

When we live before our children in truth, we equip them for life in Christ. As they see us take authority over our enemies, and as we lead them to pray through the Five Keys, we give them an understanding of the power they have been given over their own enemies. When we experience spiritual freedom in response to a simple command, we really understand how an evil spirit influences us. The same will be true for our children. The family of faith has no need to hide spiritual realties, for we want the children to experience the power of God so their faith

---

[5] This is said with a calm voice of authority and without anxiety or fear. In the same way that a parent who expects to be obeyed says directly and firmly, "Son, it's time to go to bed," you can say, "Anger, it's time to leave."

moves out of the realm of simple head knowledge or intellectual assent into the realm of true knowledge of God.

See Testimony #3 in Appendix A for another example of praying with a child.

Question #10

I have heard you say not to dig during a session, but I have noticed you ask many questions. Can you clarify?

Answer

When we interview someone, we want to help them to tell their story, uncover what is hidden, and name their enemies. We help by asking questions that are natural to the conversation they have initiated. We do not ask about sins or secrets unrelated to what they have shared; we do not operate out of curiosity. Instead, we open doors for people to go through. We do not go where we are not welcomed. If you communicate love, respect, and understanding, you will be welcomed. If the person feels safe and not judged, the doors to their heart are open wide.

Further Reflection

You will want to provide a safe environment. This is why it is so strategic for people to have some understanding of Unbound either by reading the book, attending a conference, or by receiving individual instruction before you begin the interview. Knowledge and familiarity set the context for the conversation and enable you to walk side by side with the one who came for prayer. In this scenario, you are not the interrogator; rather, you're a friend, a fellow believer walking with them just as someone once walked with you.

Even a word of knowledge (a revelation) can be invasive and could potentially shut someone down. If you "get" the word *rape* or "see" a child being beaten, do not abruptly say, "I am getting the word *rape*" or "I see a child being beaten." We recommend you use what may be a revelation from God as a guidepost. Since you now expect it to come up, you can ask about it in the context of other questions. It is very possible you have received a revelation but not its meaning.

It could be that fear entered the person when they saw a movie or perhaps their mother was raped and they always carried a fear of rape. If you ask, expecting to hear they were raped, you may be asking in a way that steers them away from the actual root.

Imagine a battlefield with many easily recognizable enemies on the frontlines. As you look closely, you will see there are many more enemies positioned behind the ones you see—ones that are camouflaged, looking like the scenery. These are not so easy to recognize. First, help people to see and name the enemy that is right before them. Then, through questions, help them to recognize and acknowledge the ones that were obscured and hidden. (See "Grouping of Spirits," p. 61)

Following the first three keys, the command is given and the battlefield is swept clean. It is then that what is under the trees and behind the frontlines will likely appear. Once their cover is taken away, the person is free to see what was buried. You will not have to dig them up. Often, people who are self-aware or have been to a good spiritual director or therapist may tell you what is on the battlefield; others may need more help to catch on.

When I say do not dig, it is because I encourage you to avoid depending on human means and natural understanding. Instead, have confidence in the Lord and His faithfulness to work through the Five Keys. Bring to the interview all you have learned about human nature, patterns of behavior, and how the enemy deceives, but trust in the Lord to do the work.

Question #11

How do I screen people who request ministry?

Answer

After you begin an UNBOUND prayer ministry, you may get many calls requesting prayer. If you do not know the person or if you do not know the person who referred them to you, it is a good idea to start with a mini interview over the phone to get some basic information. What should you listen for? Here are a few suggestions:

- How did they hear about your ministry and UNBOUND? This is a great question to start with because it gives you an idea of the background from which they come.

- Have they read UNBOUND, gone to a conference, or heard the teaching on the Five Keys? This is important because you want them to know your approach to the ministry session so they are prepared and can cooperate. You want to avoid unrealistic or false expectations. If they have not done any of the above, ask them to read UNBOUND. Reading the book ensures they are willing to invest in their own healing and is one sign they will "do whatever it takes."

- Did they relate personally to the book or to the conference teaching? What have they already done to get help? Are they in a church? What does their pastor think? Do they have a relationship with mature Christian friends or are they in a small group that will help them continue to grow? Could their pastor or friend come with them to a session so they can follow up on what is done? Are they already working with a healing ministry, their pastor, or a therapist? The enemy desires to isolate people, so from the beginning, point people to find healthy, loving Christian relationships. If they do not have any healthy, supportive Christian relationships, this may be a warning signal that they are not in a place to receive UNBOUND prayer. In this case, encourage them to seek out those relationships before coming for prayer.

- Have they received deliverance prayer before? This question helps you understand what they have already experienced and what issues they have already worked on. It also gives you the opportunity to highlight the difference between UNBOUND and other deliverance ministries.

- Have they received UNBOUND prayer before? If so, did they feel free? If people did experience freedom previously, this gives you a "jumping off point" for deeper freedom.

- What are the current issues going on in their life? Are they involved in ongoing counseling or therapy? Are they taking medication?

This is good to know before going in, and it helps show if they are dealing with any issues or mental illness in a healthy way. Encourage them if they are. Counseling and therapy are positive and shouldn't deter you from praying with them.

✢ Do they have past or present involvement in the occult? It is good to be aware of any occult involvement ahead of time, but again, this will not deter you from praying with them.

What if you do not feel confident your team can handle this person and their issues? One leader confessed, "I worry over that kind of decision; after I turn someone away, I wonder whether I was acting out of fear or laziness, if I decided too quickly, if I sought the Lord on it enough, if maybe I could have done something to help a person in distress and chose not to." This is difficult. You cannot help everyone, but you can help anyone the Lord sends to you. So how do you make your decision? Remain dependent on His grace. As you ask Him humbly what to do, expect to hear from Him. Know that as you enter into His presence, you can put your doubts, unbelief, and fears aside and listen. Trust God's people to Him and trust Him to lead you as you make the best decisions you can. Use these situations as a motivation for prayer for greater wisdom and authority. Remember, the more people you help find freedom in Christ, the more you will be able to notice red flags.

One obvious red flag is that the individual has read *Unbound* but shows no comprehension of the Five Keys. If they add to their lack of comprehension by acting powerless, speaking negatively about others who have tried to help them, or are continually demanding to find a holy person to drive out the demon, you can suggest they find someone else with more experience. If you know a professional counselor who could help them overcome these hindrances to accepting the Five Keys, you may want to refer them. I am fortunate to have a psychiatrist I can call on if I am not sure a particular individual will respond well to ministry. He holds a phone interview with the person and recommends either that we go ahead or, at times, that the individual have therapy or medication as a prerequisite for a session. He is very aware of psychological conditions that may mimic the demonic or create a situation of irrational fear (paranoia). It is important for you to know that if medication is not correctly balanced, it will hinder a person from engaging in the ministry.

If you do not have that kind of access to a professional and you are not sure if the person is a candidate, you may find guidance in questions you ask yourself: Have you asked the Lord to help you and guide you? What is He saying to you? How much experience do you have? Are you just beginning or do you have years of experience with the Five Keys? How much time do you have to give to someone right now? Do you have a team leader you can talk to who will help you decide? Do you have a pastor or someone with more experience to consult? Would you have time to meet with the person so you can better evaluate and help them get some other assistance and arrange a time to pray for them later if they want? Are there other resources, groups, ministries, or a trusted therapist you can recommend to them?

You should never enter into a session because you have been pressured to do so. So if after you have prayed you still have reservations, trust they are from the Lord. As you grow in experience, you will be better able to help people with a wide range of issues.

Further Reflection

If you are just getting started, it is ideal to start with people who are part of your local church community whom you are certain are seeking the Lord and are in healthy relationships. You will learn a great deal at this level. If you continue to serve, however, you will get calls from people who are severely demonized, emotionally troubled, or psychologically disturbed. Sometimes a man or woman will be experiencing physical attacks and mental torment by the demonic. Do they appear stable or unstable? Are there indicators that tell you they have been pursuing the Lord during this crisis? Do you believe the Lord sent them? If yes, go for it! By asking them what they learned from reading *Unbound,* you will know if they are ready to participate or if they are confused and want somebody to do this for them. If they have already been pursuing their freedom, then they may better understand this is a process more than a quick fix. (If someone has called you on behalf of someone else who needs ministry, make sure you have the person call you before seeing them. And if you are going to see a child, make sure you have the time to minister to the parents and that they are open to such ministry. Some parents want you to fix their kids and the children may want to be free, but it is unlikely they will hold their freedom if the parents are not seeking freedom as well. It is always best to have the parents present when you minister to a child.)

When you meet for a ministry session with someone whom you have hesitated to minister to, do not promise you will lead them through the Five Keys. Instead, you may wish to give them guidelines on what would be some preliminary steps to a complete UNBOUND session. If you do not know the person, it would be wise to have them sign a release form. This form will safeguard all who minister with you and make clear to the one coming for prayer what they can expect. I realize this may sound daunting. Be encouraged, though. If you follow the guidelines and do not try too hard to set the person free but instead listen, love, and lead them to the Lord, it is unlikely you will do harm and very probable you will help them on their journey to freedom. I do get reports of severely damaged people who have been helped in significant ways through the Five Keys. Remember, the Lord is leading you and teaching you through the people He sends you. Do not expect He will be jumping you directly from an introductory lesson to a graduate level course. As you move in compassion, seek the Lord for wisdom, have confidence He will lead you, and turn even your mistakes into victories. Pride comes before a fall, so humble yourself and He will protect you.

QUESTION #12

How do I know if someone has serious mental illness? Should I minister to him or her?

ANSWER

I asked Edward McGonigle, MD, a psychiatrist who is part of our local UNBOUND ministry team, to help us with this one. According to Dr. Ted, the answers to the following questions will give you a good sense of whether the person is seriously ill:

- Is the person unable to tell a coherent story? Do they speak in a state of confusion?

- Does the person have an obvious inability to focus and concentrate?

- Is the person exhibiting any paranoid delusions? (*Delusion* is defined as a "fixed, false belief.")

- Is the person's appearance generally disheveled or unkempt?

- Do you feel manipulated or strongly pulled into their story during the interview?

No one of these alone is a determining factor, but taken together they are good indicators. If you see these things, you may ask the person, "Has any doctor ever diagnosed you?" or "Are you or have you ever been on medications for mental health?" The answers you get will help you understand.

Dr. Ted writes:

> Serious mental illness would be indicated by the following diagnoses: Schizophrenia, serious forms of bipolar disorder, obsessive-compulsive disorder (OCD), serious forms of depression, serious forms of post-traumatic stress disorder (PTSD), borderline personality disorder (BPD), or dissociative identity disorder (DID)/multiple personality disorder (MPD).
>
> Of note, BPD and DID/MPD are sometimes related to satanic ritual abuse.
>
> If someone tells you he is bipolar or OCD, ask yourself if this is a true diagnosis or not. Many people say "I'm OCD" but really only have obsessive-compulsive personality traits. When the true condition exists, the most critical question (apart from "are you under the care of a psychiatrist or therapist?") is how much a person sees the condition as part of his identity.

If serious mental illness exists, should you minister with the Unbound model? Keep in mind that you can always pray for someone's healing if they would like you to. If you feel led to minister to a person with a serious mental illness, you should be experienced in

UNBOUND and *proceed within the context of an ongoing relationship with them*. You should also be in communication with those who have medical or spiritual authority in their life. Deliverance should not be seen as a quick fix or be offered outside of the context of their life of faith, but if administered faithfully, it may offer them significant help.

You may have heard stories of people who had spectacular deliverance from spirits that mimicked mental illness. This is not the norm. It would be a disservice to minister to any person expecting a quick fix. You can imagine how much rejection, embarrassment, humiliation, and hurt one may carry by being treated as an outcast. They do not need one more experience of abandonment and broken promises. They need a friend. The best context for ministry is within an ongoing relationship where trust has been built. If you understand the simplicity of the Five Keys and how natural they are to the Christian life, you can confidently go through doors that are opened in the conversation. If you do not have such a friendship with the one who wants prayer, it may be better for you to teach someone who is in relationship with them. In that case, you may assist in prayer. Dr. Ted says it this way:

> It may not be possible to get deeply into deliverance with someone who has a serious mental health condition. At the very least, love him extra well. Respect him extra well. Be patient! Be compassionate! The person may benefit most from someone who is able to truly listen to him. Listen to him without fear. So many in his life are filled with fear and uncertainty; it will be a powerful testimony that you are not afraid.
>
> It is also important to speak in concrete terms and repeat yourself when getting permission to pray and while actually praying. Common "root issues" are rejection, abandonment, and self-hatred. If the Spirit guides you away from praying all five keys, attempt to help him with forgiveness and a deeper understanding of the authority of Jesus in his life.

If the root cause of the mental illness is the work of an evil spirit, the UNBOUND approach is very similar. Do what Dr. Ted suggests: Be a friend and listen. Bring them to understand the Good News and help them to verbally commit their life to Jesus and enter a Christian environment. Then, as your relationship develops, teach or lead them to pronounce forgiveness and to renounce and command that which they have renounced to leave. Follow every layer of freedom with the blessing of their true identity as a child of God. Be patient; you can only go as far as the person is willing and you can do only what God has prepared for you to do. (If demonic manifestations are not provoked yet continually interfere, find someone with greater expertise with whom you can consult.)

QUESTION #13

Are there limits to confidentiality?

ANSWER

Confidentiality is absolutely essential to UNBOUND ministry. If one person believes they have been betrayed, then many others will not come for help. If they come with doubt and fear, they may not have the kind of trust that is necessary to share deeply. That said, there *may* be limits. If there are, it is imperative that you be upfront about what those limits are. You should not invite someone to share something you feel you would need to report.

What are some possible limits to confidentiality? The first limit is in the area of conscience. If the person is a danger to themselves or to others, you cannot send them on their way with a simple blessing. They came for prayer because they wanted help. Make sure they get the help they need. Begin by urging them to call their doctor or psychiatrist. Then you might want to say, "I will call you to see you have done it." Next, you may tell them that if they have not followed through, you will do something more to protect them. Let them know what that something will be. If you feel they should not leave your session without help in place, you may want to call 911 yourself. In all your responses and actions, remember to love the person well. The second limit to confidentiality has to do with the law. Many states in the USA, as well as many countries, have established laws to protect children from abuse. The government trains people who work with children to look for the warning signs of child abuse and to report suspicions to the proper authorities. In my state, as well as others, these people are designated as *mandated reporters*. They may be doctors, social workers, teachers, school nurses, or daycare providers. When professionals (or volunteers) working with children *function in their role*, they are required to report information about child abuse. When they are not in their role, they are not mandated, but they should still use their discretion to protect children. This is very reasonable. The purpose of the law is prevention and protection.

In some states, the laws are more restrictive and the attorneys general have interpreted the law even more tightly, requiring all to report suspicions of abuse whether functioning in or out of official roles. UNBOUND ministry goes on across the states and even around the world. You need to find out what the law is in your locality and know what your responsibility is. Then you need to find a way to let people know the limits of your confidentiality and not let someone share with you information they do not want you to be responsible for. This can be done in a release form or in a gentle and loving warning during a session.

You also need to have a policy on how team members and leaders share information when they seek advice. Whether such sharing is always done anonymously or by securing the individual's permission is up to you.

CHAPTER 12

Why Unbound Differs From Other Deliverance Models

QUESTION #14
Why do you not speak the "blood of Jesus" in your battle with demons?

ANSWER:

We do not battle demons. Instead, we help people take hold of the freedom they have been given in Christ. Our focus is always on helping the individual Christian take a stand against the tactics of the devil rather than confronting demons themselves. We follow the teaching of Ephesians 6 and encourage each man and woman to walk in truth and in faith. We have found that when lies and unbelief are exposed and renounced, the evil spirits that animated those lies are put to flight.

FURTHER REFLECTION

One reason the "blood of Jesus" is used in deliverance ministry is that it—along with commands in the name of Jesus, reading Scriptures, declaring the truth, using holy objects, and ritual prayers—can torment the demons. Unfortunately, demons may express this pain and bring torment in the Christian's body.

We are not interested in provoking demons. We want to minister to each person with as little spiritual distraction as possible. We teach people to observe what is going on within and to tell us. We do not believe a Christian should give themselves over to a spirit that is afflicting them as though allowing it to manifest is the only way to discover its identity and drive it out. How then can we know if any deliverance takes place if there is no manifestation? The answer is very simple. The person tells us the bondage is broken and we know by the fruit manifested in their life. We do not need to know if every area of spiritual bondage has been dealt with because deliverance is a process and God always has more freedom for His sons and daughters.

When a deliverance ministry provokes demons or "goes after" a demon, the possibility of abuse skyrockets. This plays right into the devil's hands. The devil wants to discredit ministry and undermine the Christian's belief in God's sovereignty, His fatherly love, and the protection He gives to His children. Abuses I have witnessed over the years led me to seek the Lord for a simple and safe approach to deliverance ministry. When I wrote *Unbound: a Practical Guide to Deliverance*, I felt the Lord wanted us to keep our model of deliverance straightforward, very close to the Scriptures, simple enough to be reproducible, and to avoid adding anything from other ministries unless it proved necessary. The context for UNBOUND ministry is evangelization, the proclamation of the kingdom. Therefore, when a man or woman wants to surrender to Jesus, teach them how to live in freedom as His disciple and how to seek the Spirit's help to win the spiritual battles they will encounter.

If, instead of evangelization (or what some call discipling), a ministry focuses on demons, the Christian may be hurt. Suddenly, they and their problems have been upstaged by a battle between the minister and demons. In the UNBOUND model, you avoid this danger by remaining focused on the individual. UNBOUND is a ministry of love in which you walk alongside a person as Jesus leads them to the heart of the Father, the place of deepest healing.

Though many people hope for deliverance and even read books about it, they never pray for it because it seems too complex or dangerous. UNBOUND's very simplicity equips people all over the world to pray confidently for others to be set free. The UNBOUND model has been reproduced over many years in many countries and cultures and we are continually seeking to present the message in ways that make it accessible to the whole church. (For further reflection on this question, see related testimony in Appendix A, page 175.)

Again, why do we not speak "the blood of Jesus" as we minister? It is because we do not drive demons out by tormenting them. Instead, we address the entryways, close the doors, break the legal right, and know the demons must leave when so commanded in the name of Jesus.

Question # 15

Why don't you teach people to bind the spirits when praying for someone to be liberated?

Answer

Jesus has already bound the spirits in the lives of believers and we exercise our faith according to that truth.

Further Reflection

There is nothing wrong with beginning a deliverance session with the binding of spirits. Many of those who minister in deliverance use the form "I bind you (or this spirit) in the name of Jesus" to prevent or minimize manifestations of the enemy. They believe this declaration will hinder the enemy from interfering with the deliverance session or that it will prevent the enemy from working in the individual until the time the person is delivered. Indeed, binding spirits can be very helpful when a person appears to have lost control to a demonic manifestation. However, I believe it is a mistake to elevate the practice to the level of essential formula, for we can address manifestations in other, equally effective ways.

Since we know the Lord has bound the fallen angels (Jude 6) and Jesus holds the keys of death and death's domain through His own death and resurrection (Revelation 1:18), I do not speak a declaration of binding but focus instead on helping the person take control of their mind and body. I learned from Pablo Bottari to speak directly to the person: "John, take control of your mind and your body and open your eyes." The real issue is not the presence of a demon but the need for the one who has come for prayer to stand in their identity and use the will

God has given them. They must agree with the truth proclaimed in the Scriptures, the truth that Jesus is *Christus Victor* (Ephesians 1:19-23).

The key here for both the minister and the one who has come for prayer is that their beliefs must match up with revealed truth. The enemy can work in a believer's life because there is some level of agreement within the person that gives the enemy access. Therefore, as the person breaks the areas of agreement with the enemy through repentance, forgiveness, and renunciation (the first three keys of the UNBOUND model), the enemy, who has been bound by Jesus, is now prevented from acting in those areas of their life. Satan's ability to influence is broken. When you give the command "I break the power of the spirits renounced and command them to leave," the believer can enter into their inheritance in the heart of their Father.

In Mark 3:27, Jesus uses a parable from the Jewish practice of exorcism to point to the greater truth of His divine work. We read, "But no one can enter a strong man's house and plunder his goods, unless he first binds the strong man; then indeed he may plunder his house." Jesus is the One who has entered the house of the devil, or "strong man." He entered the kingdom of darkness and robbed Satan of what belonged to him through our sin. He paid the price for our redemption, and now we have been delivered from the kingdom of darkness and brought into the kingdom of the beloved Son. Rather than giving a formula or a universal method to follow, Jesus in this parable hints at what St. Paul's letter to the Colossians makes clear: that our chains have already been broken by what Jesus has already done for us.[1]

---

[1] Consulting on this topic with Mary Healy, author of *The Gospel of Mark (Catholic Commentary on Sacred Scripture)*, she put it this way: "When Jesus speaks of 'binding the strong man' in Mark 3:27, He is referring to his death and resurrection, through which He is able to conquer the power of Satan and break his hold over human beings. The parable is in the context of a discussion about exorcisms but also has a broader meaning that applies to all His works of healing, forgiveness, and liberation from the power of evil. Jesus is saying the reason He has power to cast out demons and free human beings from oppression is because He is about to subdue Satan himself through His paschal mystery. It would be illegitimate to conclude from the parable that all exorcisms must include a 'binding' formula. All exorcisms must, however, include faith in Jesus' victory over Satan through His cross and resurrection."

Why Unbound Differs From Other Deliverance Models

We read in Colossians 2:11-15:

In Him also you were circumcised with a circumcision made without hands, by putting off the body of flesh in the circumcision of Christ; and you were buried with Him in baptism, in which you were also raised with Him through faith in the working of God, who raised Him from the dead. And you, who were dead in trespasses and the uncircumcision of your flesh, God made alive together with Him, having forgiven us all our trespasses, having canceled the bond which stood against us with its legal demands; this He set aside, nailing it to the cross. He disarmed the principalities and powers and made a public example of them, triumphing over them in Him.

The battle has been won. The enemy has been tied up and humiliated. His legal access has been canceled. Now if you are to use the formula of commanding a spirit to be bound, use it knowing it is spoken as an expression of agreement with the deep reality of what God has already done.

In rare situations, I will find it necessary to give a command to the spirit: "Be quiet," or "be still," or "submit," followed by "in the name of Jesus." These commands, spoken with authority and serving the same purpose as saying "I bind you in the name of Jesus," can powerfully strengthen someone's wavering faith. Once given, I will not repeat the command but act in faith that the demon must obey, thus shifting the focus back to Jesus' sovereignty, accessed by faith, where it rightly belongs.

When we teach the UNBOUND model, we impart, in practical ways, the attitude and the faith that have been given to us. We honor those who approach binding in a different way but believe that, for us, not using the binding formula is an expression of faith. God honors our words because He knows what is in our hearts. Faith is primary; words are vital but secondary because they simply articulate the faith that is already in operation.

QUESTION #16

If Jesus has already bound the spirits and we exercise our faith according to that truth, then how should we understand "binding" in Matthew 16:19 and Matthew 18:19?

Answer

These two passages refer to church authority and discipline and do not directly instruct us about spiritual warfare. Binding and loosing can have varied meanings depending on the context.

Further Reflection

In both these passages we read: "whatever you bind on earth shall be bound in heaven, and whatever you loose on earth shall be loosed in heaven." When we consider the context of each, we see that they do not refer to spiritual warfare.

> *He said to them, "But who do you say that I am?" Simon Peter replied, "You are the Christ, the Son of the living God." And Jesus answered him, "Blessed are you, Simon Bar-Jonah! For flesh and blood has not revealed this to you, but My Father who is in heaven. And I tell you, you are Peter, and on this rock I will build my church, and the powers of death shall not prevail against it. I will give you the keys of the kingdom of heaven, and whatever you bind on earth shall be bound in heaven, and whatever you loose on earth shall be loosed in heaven."*
>
> Matthew 16:15-19

The word *binding* has to do with forbidding, and the word *loosing* has to do with permitting or allowing. In this passage, the keys of the kingdom refer to authority. In context, authority is given to Peter, who has received the revelation from the Father about the true identity of Jesus. Peter was given authority to teach and make binding decisions (rabbis were said to have made "binding" interpretation of the law). Heaven stands behind the exercise of God-given authority. Binding is not always negative. It is a good thing to be bound to the Lord, His will, and His people.

In the Matthew 18 passage, the phrase occurs in the context of church discipline:

> *So it is not the will of My Father who is in heaven that one of these little ones should perish. If your brother sins against you, go and tell him his fault, between you and him alone. If he listens to you, you have gained your brother. But if he does not listen, take one or two others along with you, that every word may be confirmed by the evidence of two or three*

Why Unbound Differs From Other Deliverance Models

witnesses. If he refuses to listen to them, tell it to the church; and if he refuses to listen even to the church, let him be to you as a Gentile and a tax collector. Truly, I say to you, whatever you bind on earth shall be bound in heaven, and whatever you loose on earth shall be loosed in heaven. Again I say to you, if two of you agree on earth about anything they ask, it will be done for them by My Father in heaven. For where two or three are gathered in My name, there am I in the midst of them.

Matthew 18:14-20

Here, binding may refer to including and excluding members of the community, or forgiving and not forgiving sins (see John 20:23), or laying down rules and making exceptions. This does not mean the principle of binding and loosing cannot be drawn upon in other realms of life, like prayer or spiritual warfare. But like Peter, the authority you carry begins with the revelation of Christ. Your words and actions, based on revelation and empowered by the Holy Spirit, are what enable you to set the captives free. When someone is released from bondage (they are loosed), it is the work of heaven on earth. What happens on earth affects the spiritual battle that is going on in heavenly realms. The power the enemy has in heavenly places came through man's sin and rebellion. As the believer is made more like Christ and as they deny the enemy access to their heart, Satan's presence is displaced in heavenly realms.

Question #17

Why don't you teach people to pray a cleansing prayer after ministry?

Answer

A prayer of cleansing is typically a prayer to break free (be cleansed) of any evil spirits that may have attached themselves to a person during ministry. In the context of Unbound ministry, a cleansing prayer is rarely necessary. You will not want to pray in a way that shifts the focus onto evil spirits or is inconsistent with our belief that spirits must find something in a believer to attach to. Instead, pray according to our teaching and according to the faith that has been given to you.

Further Reflection

Prayer is essential. Both before and during ministry, humble yourself before the Lord and ask for what you need. Before you intercede, give thanks and praise to the One who is the deliverer and pray for greater anointing, deeper faith, humility, and for release of the captives. It is important to be aware of the vital connection between what you believe and what you pray. In the Gospel of Mark, Jesus is asked by His disciples why they could not cast out a demon from a boy (Mark 9:28). His response is, "This kind cannot be driven out by anything but prayer" (vs. 29), but in the Gospel of Matthew, Jesus' response appears to be different: "Then the disciples came to Jesus in private and asked, 'Why couldn't we drive it out?' He replied, 'Because you have so little faith'" (Matthew 17:19-20 NIV). In one place, Jesus speaks about prayer (and fasting); in another, He says it is because of a lack of faith. Is His response actually different?

Faith is your grace-filled response to the revelation of God. You received power in your conversion, but it is through your faith you release the power to take hold of the freedom you have been given. Prayer is also a response—a response to God's initiative in your life. "We love, because He first loved us" (1 John 4:19). In like manner, you pray because He first revealed Himself to you. Prayer is an expression of faith. Prayer expresses what you believe and faith is expressed through prayer. (I examine the connection between faith and prayer further in *Resisting the Devil,* pp. 80-81.)

Your prayers should also reflect your struggle to believe what God has revealed. The Lord's Prayer, for example, expresses both what we actually believe and what we all struggle to believe each day. I have not written a prayer to use following UNBOUND ministry because I prefer you use Luke 10 as a model. I prefer you struggle to believe Jesus' words that nothing will harm you as you minister in His authority.

> *The seventy-two returned with joy and said, "Lord, even the demons submit to us in Your name." He replied, "I saw Satan fall like lightning from heaven. I have given you authority to trample on snakes and scorpions and to overcome all the power of the enemy; nothing will harm you. However, do not rejoice that the spirits submit to you, but rejoice that your names are written in heaven." At that time Jesus,*

full of joy through the Holy Spirit, said, "I praise You, Father, Lord of heaven and earth, because You have hidden these things from the wise and learned, and revealed them to little children. Yes, Father, for this was Your good pleasure."

Luke 10:17-21 (NIV)

Your first response should be to return to Jesus with rejoicing and share in His pleasure and His joy. As you humble yourself in praise and gratitude for the privilege of participating in His ministry, remember that your success is all by His grace. Pay attention to His words, "Nothing will harm you." Those who minister regularly have learned to stand on these words and rarely have to pray them. Those who are new to the UNBOUND model may have to pause to remember, "This is a ministry of love; I have been helping a person respond to Jesus and enter into the power of the kingdom. This has been the work of the Lord through me; He has come to set the captives free." You are His instrument and sometimes just a bystander as you watch the Holy Spirit work in a person's life.

Faith and prayer are like two sides of the same coin. Your conviction of truth can be expressed in an attitude of heart, a conversation with others, or a time of prayer. Faith is expressed in prayer but is not limited to prayer. Remembering and believing can be as important as saying a prayer.

Francis MacNutt, well known in healing ministry, has written a binding prayer and a cleansing prayer that is used by thousands of people. You can read about these prayers in his spring of 1997 newsletter, which can be found at www.christianhealingmin.org. As a teacher, Francis wrote these prayers to pass along his wealth of experience. In the context of his ministry, he found these prayers helpful. He writes, however,

> In no way do we want to get into a kind of legalism that implies you have to pray with these particular categories or your prayer won't work. Our prayer is just an example of how you can pray, but if you come up with another prayer, which is better for you, that's fine.
>
> *The Healing Line,* Spring 1997

Francis MacNutt's prayers mirror his particular approach to deliverance ministry and his understanding of the faith that has empowered his ministry and opened the doorway to God's grace. The question is whether these prayers or others like them fit the context of Unbound ministry. Do they reflect the faith that is being expressed in an Unbound session?

While we do not want to fall into the trap of thinking that Unbound is the only way, at the same time we do have reasons for our model. Those reasons are based on what the Lord has taught us. We do not expect others to have the same emphasis in ministry, but we caution you against raising forms of prayer and particular approaches to deliverance, be it Unbound or any other, to the level of principles that are universal when they are not. Jesus is the deliverer and you cannot limit the means of His redeeming work. Whether you pray a particular prayer, at a particular time, in a particular way or you do not is not the vital issue. "The only thing that counts is faith expressing itself in love" (Galatians 5:6 NIV). It is by your fruit that you are known.

You may want to re-read and study the questions and answers in Chapter 10 if you struggle with this. Remember, you live by faith. Faith deepens in the Lord's disciples over time as they listen and obey. I no longer have to fight some battles because I stand on the victories I have already won (through Him). There will always be new territory to take, new battles to fight, and a deeper faith to be uncovered.

Question #18

I do not think I will be comfortable praying for deliverance without using a cleansing and a binding prayer. Does this mean I cannot participate in Unbound *ministry teams?*

Answer

If you wish to use the Unbound model and continue using prayers you are used to praying, there are two options: You may pray those prayers silently or you may pray them with a team member who shares your conviction before a person arrives and after they leave. If you merge your own approach with some of what you have learned from the Unbound model, we ask you do not call what you are doing

Unbound ministry. Simply explain what you are doing. For example, "We are using the five key of Unbound with some variations." Or simply call what you are doing what you have always called it.

Further Reflection

We are always delighted when anyone uses what we teach to set the captives free. We support you in serving the Lord in union with the faith you have received. We have no desire to be critical or to be a hindrance to anyone successfully using other approaches to ministry.

We also want to be faithful to the gift the Lord has entrusted to us. We need to be faithful to the core of what we have been given, knowing others will add to it. Some will improve it as they adapt it to their situation and others will distort it. It is our hope that those who teach Unbound ministry by word or example will understand the power of its simplicity before adapting it. We believe understanding each of the keys and their interrelationship is critical to training the legions of men and women who are needed to meet the growing need of those looking for true freedom. We hope you and many like you can be part of releasing this gift by modeling the Five Keys of Unbound.

As you use the Unbound model, you may find your opinion changes over time. A number of current leaders regularly prayed the cleansing prayer after each session when they began using the Unbound model for ministry. After I shared with them my thoughts and offered Luke 10 as a model, they confessed that they did find the cleansing prayer inconsistent with the rest of the ministry—they simply never thought of not saying it. They quickly understood and took up a new approach.

Question #19

I have years of experience in confrontational deliverance. Help me make the transition to the Unbound model.

Answer

It is true, the Unbound model of deliverance is very different from a model that is confrontational or uses elements of exorcism. If you are used to that model, Unbound will be a big change. Let me use an example to help you think about the change. Recently, I prayed with a young man who was burdened by a sense of oppression. While praying, I had a picture of a man who was getting beat up in a boxing ring. My instinct was to pray he would fight back. But I felt a check within. I found myself saying he was in the wrong arena and needed to move to a different ring.

UNBOUND is like a new ring. This may be a new arena of spiritual warfare for you. As you move to this new arena, you may find a new set of weapons is required. You may find it hard to understand why some things that are so important to the battle in one arena are not necessary in another. As you leave old weapons behind, you must also learn new things in this new arena. This can be difficult. I once trained a woman who was quite experienced in giving spiritual direction. Because of her training, it took her sitting through the powerful deliverance of three people in a row before she was able to see what was happening before her eyes: the Holy Spirit was bringing up and healing in minutes what could take years of counseling to uncover.

In UNBOUND ministry, the Five Keys of repentance and faith, forgiveness, renunciation, authority, and the Father's blessing interweave healing and deliverance together. You will place your emphasis on an interview and on listening carefully to a believer's story in light of these five keys. With permission, you will lead the individual through each of the keys in order. Repentance, forgiveness, and renunciation close the doors the Christian has opened to the enemy and cancel any legal right of access to their life. The command then directs every spirit they have renounced—and all related spirits—to depart. You will then conclude with the Father's blessing.

What do you need to make the transition? You will need a growing understanding of how these five keys work together. This will come with experience, study, and reflection. You will also need to be willing to be inadequate, to be in the place of not knowing, relying not on what you know but trusting the One who does know. You need to have a longing in your heart for more and a faith to know you will have all you need whenever it's needed. Close to ten years ago, I wrote, "If there is anything I wish to grow in, it is the ability…to discern the area of deepest need and speak something that God sees in the person, something at the core of his being that he understands and knows but has yet to own, because it has never been spoken... Always remember the Father is passionate to bless His children. Sometimes we just need to get out of the way and ask God to speak to them" (UNBOUND, pp. 206-207). Fortunately, the Father is *still* passionate to free His children. He will do it with you if you set your face to serve Him in this way.

QUESTION #20

I am a trained counselor. Is there a way for me to use UNBOUND *in my practice?*

ANSWER

Counselors, therapists, psychologists, and psychiatrists may have special trouble when they are introduced to UNBOUND, for their years of training have ingrained into them either a "medical" or "psychological" model. UNBOUND is a spiritual model. When I train a therapist, I usually tell them to be patient with themselves and that it may take them more time to learn UNBOUND than someone with little ministry experience. They have already gained wisdom God has used to help others; they have already used their gift to great benefit. It is not surprising that they struggle to set it aside in order to work with an entirely different model. However, the benefits of UNBOUND are most clearly seen when all five keys are used without mixing them with other approaches to therapy.

What should you do if you are convinced UNBOUND offers hope for your clients or your patients? Be wise. Some therapists bring principles of UNBOUND into their therapy but do not follow the model. Others, understanding the power of an UNBOUND session, will continue to help their clients as they have learned to do but, at an appropriate time, will offer the client the opportunity for UNBOUND ministry apart from their regular sessions. Keeping regular therapy and UNBOUND ministry separate helps prevent a weakening of either the traditional approach or the UNBOUND model.

If you already serve in a "helping" or "healing" profession, you have been blessed with access to your client's heart that most of us do not have. Honor that access by seeking the Lord for wisdom.

Question #21

Do you always pray in the name of Jesus? What if I am ministering to a Hindu or a Muslim or a Jew?

Answer

I always use the name of Jesus. If I were praying with a non-Christian, I would rejoice in the opportunity to share (even a few words) with them about Jesus (as I do when praying for a baptized Christian who has not personally encountered the Savior). I would not require them to believe Jesus is Savior and Lord for me to pray to Him, but I would explain the power of God is released through Jesus and He has authority over every enemy that can be named. "Therefore God has highly exalted him and bestowed on him the name which is above every name" (Philippians 2:9). I would also explain I have no power to help apart from Him.

Further reflection

A few people have told me that when praying with the Five Keys for a non-Christian, they have prayed in the name of God or the God of Abraham (not using the name of Jesus) and that non-believers have found some freedom. I am not surprised they experienced a level of release since everything we do is very healthy and empowering from a human perspective—and because God is love and He responds to those who come to Him with sincere hearts. He honors our faith in praying for others who do not believe or have little faith. Even if you do not use the name of Jesus, you as a believer are ministering in the person (name) of Christ.

The question to ask yourself, though, is why would you not want them to know who it is who gives them the victory over their enemies? Freedom is found in Jesus. As I say very often: "Freedom is life in the Son." The Father is revealed through the Son. Healing and deliverance are incomplete and may be unstable if they do not lead to the source of ongoing healing and deliverance. One woman writes:

> I have prayed in a children's hospital for a Hindu father of a child made quadriplegic in a car accident. He shared how "he has been having bad luck...from losing his job, to losing a finger in an accident,

to a wife in depression," and so on. I explained UNBOUND prayer briefly and then asked if he wanted prayer. He immediately said yes. I asked him if he minded me praying in the Name of Jesus because that was the Key of the Keys. He said he did not mind at all; that he needed all the help he could get.

People who know their need are often open to Jesus. Consider the lame man at the temple gate: "But Peter said (to him), 'I have no silver and gold, but I give you what I have; in the name of Jesus Christ of Nazareth, walk'" (Acts 3:6). Peter was not talking to a believer in Jesus but a Jew. Healing and deliverance in the New Testament were demonstrations of the kingdom of God that validated the claim Jesus was the Messiah and Lord. When the man received his healing, he received Jesus, in whose name his healing came.

The five keys are incomplete unless we lead the person to the Father. There is only one way to know the Father and that is through the Son. May the following passage remind you of the immeasurable greatness of His power at work in us who believe:

> *I do not cease to give thanks for you, remembering you in my prayers, that the God of our Lord Jesus Christ, the Father of glory, may give you a spirit of wisdom and of revelation in the knowledge of Him, having the eyes of your hearts enlightened, that you may know what is the hope to which He has called you, what are the riches of His glorious inheritance in the saints, and what is the immeasurable greatness of His power in us who believe, according to the working of His great might which He accomplished in Christ when He raised him from the dead and made Him sit at His right hand in the heavenly places, far above all rule and authority and power and dominion, and above every name that is named, not only in this age but also in that which is to come; and He has put all things under His feet and has made Him the head over all things for the church, which is His body, the fullness of Him who fills all in all.*
>
> Ephesians 1:16-23

We may not require assent to the gospel from a non-Christian, but we should never hide it. If we truly love the person, we will want them to know the grace of deliverance being given to them today is a doorway to greater freedom. That freedom is found in the revelation of the Father through His Son in the power of the Holy Spirit. How can they know of His love if they do not consider the price that was paid for them?

"But God shows His love for us in that while we were yet sinners Christ died for us" (Romans 5:8).

Question #22

How much should I touch someone while leading them through the keys?

Answer

A meaningful touch can be an important part of connecting with another person. We always need to be sensitive to whether or not the person is comfortable being touched, so in Unbound Ministry we make it a habit to ask permission at the conclusion of the interview stage, before we continue the session.

Further Reflection

Being touched is a fundamental need. We are created beings who yearn for connection with God and with other humans. We feel loved when someone touches our hand, gives us a hug, places a hand on our head, and so on. These touches act as a balm, providing healing for both body and spirit. Jesus often touched the sick ones who had endured years of isolation from others. For this reason, we encourage you to touch the one to whom you minister. Your touch, however, must be both appropriate and desired.

Some people have a compulsive habit of leaning on others, squeezing another's hands repeatedly, or rubbing the hand or arm of the other person. This kind of touch can be seen as invasive or even smothering. It is not appropriate. If the one who came for prayer suffered from abuse, it is especially unsuitable. Over-touching may distract the person from the healing God has for them.

In the same way, take care not to lean too close into someone's space or into their face. Avoid anything that may make the one who sought prayer uncomfortable. But remember the healing love of God can flow through your hands. Placing your hand on a shoulder while praying the Father's blessing may be just the encouragement needed. Try to minister with touch. But what if you are the one who is uncomfortable with touching another? Do not feel pressured to do so; accept your limitations.

How should you touch? First, make sure it is all right with the one who came for prayer. Ask; do not assume. Recently, Janet prayed with a young man who had been terribly abused. When she asked if she could place her hand on his arm, he said no! So she didn't. Don't be afraid to ask again later in the prayer session. When it came time for the command, Janet asked the young man a second time if she could put her hand on his head. This time, he said yes. And so she did.

Secondly, touch lightly as an expression of compassion, support, and companionship as the person takes their stand. If you are intuitive, touching can be of great help in ongoing discernment; just make sure your touch is not threatening in any way. If you hug, ask first; if you place your hand upon the individual, place it carefully and keep it still.

Thirdly, be aware that when an evil spirit goes, there may be a complete change in how the person responds to touch. At the end of the session with the young man, Janet asked if she could give him a hug. "Yes!" he said. What a sign of liberation!

Question #23

Can someone who has an extraordinary gift of discernment use the Five Keys?

Answer

Some people are used to taking a strong lead in ministry as they receive direction from the Lord. They help people through their gifts of revelation such as wisdom, prophecy, or words of knowledge. Others have extraordinary ability to discern spiritual realities. By grace, they can see things, feel things, know things, or even smell things that reveal the presence of bondage and evil or the presence of God and the working of His Spirit and angels. But they cannot always pass their gift on to others. One very gifted woman told me she had been doing what I was doing for thirty years but had never had a way of teaching others to do it. She could only suggest they watch her. After watching her minister, a few were able to go out and help others, but most left still unequipped (though amazed at how God worked through her).

I believe that as these leaders understand the Five Keys, they will be able to better interpret the revelation they receive and will have increased insight into how to lead a person to freedom. So, yes, the Five Keys add to the ministry of one with the gift of discernment.

Further Reflection

If you spend time listening and loving another person through the screen of the Five Keys, you are making room for the supernatural. Gifts of discernment are from the Spirit. They are a reminder to all of us that God can work through us in ways we do not currently understand or experience. On occasion, as I have been in the middle of a very brief prayer encounter, the Lord has given me supernatural direction. It happens something like this: I listen as a man asks for prayer for some presenting issues. Based on the Five Keys, I ask if he struggles with unworthiness, worthlessness, or some similar lie of the enemy. I may ask if he was ever humiliated. "Yes," he says immediately, quite amazed at how I could know him so well. Now I don't really know him, but the Lord does, and I asked those particular questions because as I looked at him, I discerned from the Lord that those were the issues to deal with. My discernment was both supernatural and based on years of experience in dealing with people's patterns and leading them to the Lord. In this way, the Lord uses the Five Keys to give such revelation that freedom can come within minutes rather than in an hour or two of Unbound ministry or a year or two of counseling.

In an Unbound ministry session, pay attention to the Holy Spirit. He will reveal what the Father is doing in the person who shares. Expect revelation. But give priority to the spiritual understanding that comes through the person's words, attitude, and emotions. Insights you receive as a revelation from the Lord that do not line up with the person's sharing should take second place in the process. Believe the Holy Spirit will speak through the man or woman. If you receive a word of knowledge or an insight from the Lord, wait for Him to open the door in that direction or wait until there is an appropriate time to ask a question about that revelation. When you share the insight the Lord gave you, he will be the more encouraged and even be able to understand his own story more deeply. If you have extraordinary gifts of the Spirit, make sure you do not miss the significance of what the person is saying in your efforts to hear from the Lord. If you listen well, wait patiently, and present your revelation in the form of a question, you will be able to confirm and bring further insight into what the person is just beginning to understand.

We recognize that placing your priority on listening to the one in front of you will be a paradigm shift if you have spent years actively receiving spiritual discernment and revelation outside the context of listening to the person's story. If you wish to use the Five Keys as we teach them in UNBOUND ministry, you will need to make that shift.

Appendix Contents

Appendix A: Unbound Readings

Part 1: UNBOUND MINISTRY Testimonies **167**

Part 2: Sample Ministry Session **179**

Appendix B

Description of Ministry Documents and Tools found in Appendix B **199**

Part 1: Prayer Ministry Training Outline **201**

Part 2: Learning to Listen Practice Sheet **206**

Part 3: Discernment Article: **207**

Part 4: Samples of Related Spirits **211**

Part 5: Lies to Renounce **214**

Part 6: Developing an Unbound Ministry **218**

*Please note that online documents may be edited, removed, or added by Heart of the Father Ministries at any time.

Appendix A
UNBOUND READINGS
Part I: UNBOUND MINISTRY Testimonies

TESTIMONY #1: COMPASSION OVERCOMES FEAR
(FOLLOW-UP TO CHAPTER 4)

For many years, I had horrible nightmares and an active sense of evil that froze me with fear. I felt both helpless and a bit hopeless. Things felt even worse after my life-changing conversion, not because my experiences increased in frequency but because I was still having them.

I was in love with Jesus Christ and had placed my life in His hands. Obedience, full trust, active participation in the Sacraments and in service, long hours of prayer and adoration, and a love of reading Scripture did not take the nightmares away. I did not understand how and why I was still sensing a horrible presence oppressing me at night. Why was I still gripped by terrible fear? I felt guilty because Scripture says, "Perfect love casts away all fear." I knew in my heart that with Jesus I had nothing to fear—but I was not experiencing this reality. Jesus is perfect, His love for us is real, so if I was still afraid, it must have been my fault. There had to be something wrong with me—but what? I was failing our Lord in some way—but how? Did I not love Him enough? Did I not have enough faith? I was miserable!

One day, my husband attended a conference and brought home *UNBOUND: A Practical Guide to Deliverance* on the recommendation of a priest. As I read the book prayerfully, I felt a dark cloud lift off me. I became full of joy and knew I had found the answer to my problem. I knew my life had been changed forever and I sensed God wanted me to share this wonderful gift with others. I believed God wanted my parish priest to read UNBOUND; He wanted a deliverance ministry in our parish; and without a doubt He wanted an UNBOUND conference in my city of Vancouver, BC. I acted in obedience and everything just flowed. My parish priest read the book and agreed to a conference. I contacted Neal Lozano and together, with the support of my parish priest, we brought the ministry of UNBOUND to Vancouver and brought help to so many people.

I was hungry to learn more, hungry to get prayer for myself, but most of all I was full of compassion—a great compassion, love, and desire to help all the people who suffered just as I had suffered before finding UNBOUND. They needed to know there was an answer to their problem; they needed to experience the freedom and joy I had experienced. How could it be that nobody was shouting this message of freedom from the rooftops? After Janet prayed for me, I felt an even greater level of freedom and joy. And when our turn came to pray for others in teams, every person who came to us was deeply freed. We heard wonderful testimonies of people who had lost hope but who were finally experiencing freedom, some for the first time in their lives. In my heart, I knew this was what God wanted me to do—bring His love to all those who were hurting and bound so they could have freedom in Christ!

I continue to pray for people and continue to hear stories of freedom. It is amazing that I, who suffered so much with fear, am now in the ministry of deliverance. Our God is an awesome God! People ask what gift the Holy Spirit gave me that every prayer session should be so successful. I tell them, just as Neal says in UNBOUND, I feel an amazing love for each person God sends my way. I always tell people to read UNBOUND and do as Neal says. Don't focus on Satan; focus on the person, listen to them, listen to the Holy Spirit, and as long as they leave feeling loved, the session is successful! I can honestly say no prayer session has scared me, nothing I have heard has shocked me or caused revulsion—and I've pretty much heard it all. But I see God's little ones hurting, suffering, bound—and I feel their pain and I feel God's love for them. I do everything to communicate that love to whomever is sitting in front of me—no matter where they have been or what they have done.

I remember one woman we prayed with at the psychiatric ward in Vancouver General Hospital. She held back some important information about people she had to forgive and a few things she had to repent of and so she manifested in a very scary way as I spoke the words of authority. But in that moment, I heard Neal saying, "Love the person, call her by her name, tell her Jesus loves her," and so I did that—and it worked. She stopped manifesting and we were able to take her through repentance and forgiveness and finish the session on a high note. Was she completely free? Probably not—she had a complicated mix of mental health issues and demonic influence. But she did tell us later she felt better afterward; she felt relief and peace, and she left feeling loved and accepted and even asked for another session.

I also remember a man who began violently manifesting at the very moment he walked through our church doors for Sunday mass. With a horrible deep voice, he yelled, "Satan is here; Jesus can't help you," his words filling every corner of the church that held about seven hundred people. He repeated his shouts over and over. Everyone froze with fear. Though I had taken a break from the ministry of deliverance, I felt called to help this man. When I got to the back of the church, the man was on the floor, convulsing and growling. I felt such love and sorrow for the man and went down on my knees right next to him to ask his name and tell him Jesus loved him. Suddenly, he opened his eyes and stared at me with hatred. He growled again and said, "Jesus can't help him." I said, "Be quiet in the name of Jesus," and he closed his eyes and contorted but was quiet.

When I asked the ushers to help me get this nicely dressed parishioner (a man with friends right there in the church!) into another room, they refused. They wanted to depend on 911. As we waited, I continued to ask his name and tell him Jesus loved him. Little by little, the horrible voice quieted and the man himself was able to tell me his name. When I repeated his name and the fact that Jesus loved him, he was able to respond to my requests to sit up and then slowly stand and follow me to a chair in the foyer. He manifested periodically and said things like, "It is too late for him; there's too many of us, you can't help him." I felt greater compassion and a greater love. The thought of him being dragged off to the hospital and loaded up with drugs broke my heart since I knew he needed the help only Jesus could give. I spoke to him about God's love until the police came, handcuffed him, and led him away.

I don't claim my fears are all completely gone. I admit I am still a chicken, but my fears are the "normal," manageable kind now. On the rare occasions I have the old "scary experience," I quickly go through the Five Keys and it stops immediately. I have a remedy against the enemy so there is no more hopelessness. Best of all, when I minister to others, the compassion and love I feel for them pushes out all fear. I truly know I can do all things in Jesus Christ who strengthens me and I rejoice in God's mercy and love for me, in how He brought the gift of UNBOUND and the Lozanos into my life—and in how He has called me to this wonderful ministry of love!

TESTIMONY #2: GENERATIONAL DELIVERANCE
(FOLLOW-UP TO FAQ #9)

The following testimony is written by a mother and daughter. You will see that fear goes back at least three generations. The first part is by the daughter who lived with a fear she could not trace back to any event.

I was raised in a Spirit-filled Christian family. Compared to other people in my generation, I considered myself a strong Christian; even in high school, I followed the Lord and lived what most would label a "pure" lifestyle. As far as I can remember, I have always been a Christian and have never actively rebelled from the Lord. I cannot remember ever experiencing anything traumatic or heartbreaking. And yet fear had a total grip on my life.

One night during my freshman year in high school, while parked in a car with my father and brother outside of McDonald's, I was so overcome with fear I starting crying, begging to go home. This type of fear was common—I was constantly plagued with fear of getting injured or killed. I was so fearful that I avoided gas stations and being outside at night. Obviously, fear had an impact on my social life. Fear handicapped my ability to interact with people, so I came off as a "snob." Fear stopped me from witnessing to friends about the Lord; it even hindered my relationship with Him. I carried fear around with me everywhere even though I knew the promises the Lord had for me about fear. I had even put related Bible verses on my wall at home to constantly remind myself the Lord did not want me to be afraid, but despite my Christian walk, I could not shake the fear.

I went through one year in a secular college dealing with this fear, and I know only the grace of God carried me through that year. At the end of the year, I was given the opportunity to spend a week at a Christian camp with colleges from all over. Although I agreed to go, I dreaded the experience. I would be surrounded by people I had never met; I would be forced to participate in activities I was afraid of, such as the zip line (i.e., fear of heights). I imagined I would be miserable the whole week. But I prayed about it and I knew the Lord wanted me to go. I got to camp and found out I was right—I was miserable. When I had some time to myself, I actually crawled into my bed and cried.

I thought about the year I had just gone through and how frustrated I was over my fear and its power in my life. I remember the hopelessness and then the thought, "That's it; I give up, God. I've done everything in my power to try to shake this—now it's up to You to finish the job." And then I got up and went to dinner. Strangely, I found myself talking and laughing with a table of new acquaintances. At the time, I just thought to myself, "Wow; that was strange… I hope this lasts." Throughout the week, I engaged with people in a way I had never done before—I was able to have deep conversations and connect with people like never before. I even shocked myself when I participated in the high ropes course (think being high off the ground on wires for at least a half-hour) and didn't feel fear, though I would have been shaking in the past. Things like this happened all week. When I got home, I got up in front my church and shared how excited I was at having gone through this week unaffected by the fear that normally gripped me.

My mom heard me testify and realized a "coincidence." She had been at an UNBOUND conference that weekend. Throughout the conference, she realized that a lot of what she heard reflected the situation in my life. She decided to say a prayer for me there at the conference. The time she prayed corresponded to the time I was on my bed, crying about my problems with fear. I believe my mom was able to "stand in the gap" for me at the UNBOUND conference with the knowledge she had gained and that her prayer came alongside my desperate prayer. When she prayed, I was able to get up and go through the rest of the week with no problem at all. I was completely set free. Now I am a completely different person, my walk with the Lord has progressed so the fear no longer shackles me, and I am able to do more for the kingdom than before. Although sometimes the fear tries to attack me again, I know I can stand in the truth that I have been set free and that the Lord answered my prayer in an unexpected way!

The following is her mother's story—what happened behind the scenes.

My mother was always a person with a lot of fear in her life. When she was six months pregnant with me, my father had a car accident. Though he seriously wrecked the car, he still drove the car home and walked into the house to tell my mom about the crash. He was fine, but when my mother saw the car she was overcome by fear and slumped into a chair, unable to move. This reaction seemed to trigger labor. I was born the next day, just shy of her seventh month of pregnancy.

My husband believes the fear I grew up with came from my mother. She was always afraid of my traveling by car and I too developed the fear of going any distance in a car. I believe the fear was passed on to my daughter, and she was now worse than I was. When I went to the UNBOUND conference, I specifically asked for deliverance from fear during one of the final prayer times. While the team led me through the Five Keys, I was also praying for my daughter. I did not feel anything at the time, but since then, I realized I had a new level of victory over my fears. This occurred on a Saturday afternoon and at the very same time, my daughter was attending a Christian retreat in upstate New York.

During the week, my daughter called and said something good happened to her at the retreat. The next week at church, she said she was delivered from fear the weekend before. She said that at the retreat, she felt miserable and went to sleep. When she woke up, she felt like a new person. When she said this, I realized she had taken the nap at the same time I was receiving UNBOUND ministry. To this day, she is doing much better and knows what to do when fears come.

Appendix A

Testimony #3: Praying with Children
(FOLLOW-UP TO FAQ #9)

While driving home from the Orlando UNBOUND conference, my memory presented a clear picture. I saw myself rubbing my eight-year-old son's back and telling him how thin he was, a habit I had not even thought twice of before. I suddenly realized how this could affect his self-image and how he might associate another's touch with judgment. When I got home, I talked to him about how moms often want to see their kids have some extra meat on the bones but he was in fact exactly where he was supposed to be according to doctor's charts. He confided he had always felt guilty when I commented on his size. I apologized for making him feel bad. UNBOUND showed me how the enemy had robbed me of my freedom, and now the Lord was teaching me where my own behaviors could be affecting my son's image and freedom in Christ.

A few weeks later when I picked up my son from school, he burst into tears as soon as he entered the car. He'd had a difficult day with teachers as well as with peers. I could feel his shame and fear and sensed the prompting to ask him if he'd like to pray with the Five Keys of UNBOUND. Up until that moment, my son and I used to pray the usual formal prayers at bedtime, prayers of thanksgiving at meals, and an occasional spontaneous prayer of petition or thanks. So this was very different. I began the interview with the "Where are you stuck?" question, but he didn't understand at first until he finally said, "Oh, Mommy! You want to know what's bugging me." That became our new code word for future prayer sessions of UNBOUND.

He began telling his story about his day. As an adult, I could hear the self-justification, hurt, and anger in his trembling voice. I prayed for wisdom to find a way to ask the right questions so he might see a need for repentance. I asked if he was sure he had done absolutely nothing to make the teacher feel disrespected. He shyly answered, "Well, maybe I did keep making noises although he'd told me to be quiet." As we went through the first key we substituted the words, "In the name of Jesus, I am sorry for _____" instead of the phrase "I repent." He repented for believing he knew more than the teacher did, for being impatient with his friend at lunch, and so on. Soon more words of repentance came stumbling forward. My son admitted kids have trouble seeing where they are wrong and this was very helpful for him.

Moving into forgiveness was easy and natural. He could readily recall kids in the class who were mad at each other and had not been able to forgive others. He didn't want to end up mad forever at his best friend. I saw him begin to yawn with relief as he walked through the forgiveness key. His face was becoming more relaxed.

As we went into the third key, I explained the word *renounce* meant he was saying in the name of Jesus "I *kick out* the feeling of _____." Led by the Holy Spirit, he renounced anger, sadness, fear, stress, shame, guilt, etc. He let out deep exhalations as he "kicked out" and exclaimed, "They are leaving, Mommy! I feel lighter and happier already!" There was no need to discuss spirits. He instinctively saw the negative words of guilt, shame, and fear as "things" that were now actually leaving him. Then in a very "Mom says so" tone of authority, I said the command, "In the name of Jesus, I, John's mother, take authority and command every spirit and lie John has just kicked out to leave him right now!" We paused and John said, "Wait, mommy. I remembered something else that's really bugging me." We went through the keys about this incident and after taking authority again he exclaimed, "Mommy, it's all gone! I felt lighter and happy. I'm calm now and relaxed…I'm not afraid anymore…it's gone!" I then prayed the blessing.

My son was overjoyed. He could actually recognize he was different thanks to what Jesus had done through the prayer. We found that over the next few weeks he would ask during night prayers, "Mom, can we do UNBOUND about this thing that happened today?" The Lord was revealing unintentional remarks and actions made by family and friends that had become lies of the enemy he'd come to believe. During these prayer sessions, I had the opportunity to learn how my own actions really affected him and to seek his forgiveness for things I'd said or done which had caused fear or shame.

John began to recognize the signs of oppression and automatically took it to prayer. Within a month, my husband and I saw a tremendous change in our son. He was more carefree. He was less emotional. He was happier and doing better at school! My son also developed an even deeper empathy for his classmates. On various occasions when we carpooled, the other children in the car would be fighting with their siblings or would have crestfallen faces. John would tell them about UNBOUND and begin to explain the keys. When I spoke with these kids' parents (who belong to the same prayer group as I do), they stood by as John and I led their children through the keys. Each time the results of freedom were amazing. These parents bought the book to read and apply to themselves.

We have learned to pray with a spirit of love, listening, and receptivity! UNBOUND is not a psychological tool but a means of allowing God's grace to bring healing. It has helped to bring our family closer together and to experience the Lord's presence. I believe UNBOUND can help an entire family learn to pray together, listen to each other better, forgive each other more readily, and allow the Lord to deal with wounds before they settle into a layer of resentment that gives the enemy a stronghold in families over time.

If you ask my son John if we should pray for children with UNBOUND, he will give you a resounding yes! His desire is that all the kids in his class, together with their parents, would learn to pray this way as a family. He believes it brings Jesus to life for kids and that everyone is happier as a result. As for me, I believe praying UNBOUND with kids is a powerful experience but is most useful when we follow the airlines' instructions regarding gas masks that drop from the overhead compartment in times of an emergency: "First put on your own mask before attending to your child's!"

TESTIMONY #4: CONFRONTATIONAL OR NON-CONFRONTATIONAL DELIVERANCE
(FOLLOW-UP TO FAQ #14)

The following is a letter written by a woman in Poland to a priest who had taught her the Five Keys.

Dear Father R,

I must share an unusual experience with you.

Yesterday, I prayed with Father M for the deliverance of a lady who had been coming to him for confession and ministry for many months (every 6-8 weeks, more or less). She had been in a Hare Krishna group, and ever since leaving them, she had weird experiences—fears, depression, suicidal thoughts, blasphemous outbursts, etc. As far as I knew, everyone involved in ministry had given up on her and had sent her elsewhere. I tried to do the same, too. :-)

During our prayer yesterday, the priest poured exorcised water over her from time to time because of her responses. She had seemed to black out during the Chaplet of Divine Mercy, and would then return as from sleep and resume the prayer. She told me that she actually did not hear herself praying.

At one point, the priest simply gave up. She was not able to confess. Because she had renounced two spirits and then blacked out again, Father M renounced spirits on her behalf. When he put a stole on her shoulders, she started to tear it off, saying that it burned her. There was yet again another struggle. The priest decided that this was enough, saying that he did not know what else to do. So we closed the session, which had lasted about an hour and a half.

Because our arrangement was for her to sleep over at my place, we went back to my home. As I made tea, she started telling me a little about herself. At one point I said to her (having remembered this from one of your articles!): "Say: 'Jesus, please, prove to me that you exist. Show me that you love me.'" After a while, to my surprise, she said: "All right." And she actually spoke the words aloud to Jesus. (Before that, she had been unable to directly address Jesus.)

I'm not sure exactly how it happened, but slowly, very peacefully, with her hand in mine, I led her through the Five Keys! Through forgiveness—even though before then she would scream that she couldn't do that, that it caused her pain, that she couldn't say those words. She even forgave the man from Hare Krishna who had initiated her. (Before this, she seemed to be protecting him in a way.) Through renunciation. I gave the command. Then the blessing. I could see it all cost her dearly. Words would stick in her throat. We took breaks. But it all went on smoothly. I didn't feel any opposition. At one point, I actually stared with my mouth open wide, surprised by how strongly we felt the presence of Jesus. When we were done, she said: "Oh my, I feel so light."

She washed and went to bed immediately, before 10 pm—without any pills. In the morning, she went to confession. Father M sent me a text message: "Jesus is Lord!!! Super! I will smother you with hugs when we meet!"

She says this was the first time she had said those words herself—the renunciation and forgiveness—and took away the power from all the things that bound her, submitting them to Jesus. She had not been able to do that before. After the confession, the priest blessed her and she kissed the stole!

I am sharing this story because I was so surprised by all that was happening. For a brief moment I had thought that I was not allowed to do this, after what had happened when we prayed with the priest, especially in light of the fact that I did not have any intercessor. But earlier I had asked a friend and then later one other person to pray for protection, so with God it was sufficient! Through it all, I experienced tremendous peace and a strong sense of a smile from above. After all, it was not me who was setting the captive free.

Appendix A

Part 2: Sample Ministry Session

We are including an actual ministry session so you will gain a sense of how to listen through the words to the heart of what a person is really saying and help them identify what they need to take their stand against. No one session is typical. This session is longer because there were no time constraints as we recorded it, hoping to find a session that would be used for teaching. Editing makes his story clearer than a conversation usually is. After a brief word of welcome, Neal began.

NEAL: *Let's pray for a moment and then you can share what's going on. Simple prayer: Lord I thank you that S is here today and I ask that the Holy Spirit would lead him to be in touch with the most important things he needs to share and that I would be able to listen and understand what the Father is doing. Amen. What's going on? What's coming up that you want prayer for?*

S: Well, your conference a couple of weeks ago was an epiphany. I tried for many years to find freedom, personal healing, but I never really learned the foundation as I did at your conference. I had a wonderful blessing from my mother. She's a model in my life. I attribute everything that has been good in my life to her great example. Unfortunately, my dad, probably due to immigrant circumstances, never had a role model and never knew how to convey a blessing to me. He was the post WWII generation whose typical response to a question was "Because!" I never knew my paternal grandparents; he grew up an only child, and life had always been raw for him. As a child you don't understand "raw," but you absorb anger without truly understanding why, and anger begets anger. I was an angry child. I never had his blessing, but through a wonderful spiritual director at college I was taught that I'd have to be the agent of change and that I needed to embrace my father, which I was able to do. I was able to forgive him.

But what I learned from you and your conference is where I have been a companion for Satan in things that are still attached to me. You know, sometimes I am just gripped by anxiety, gripped by fear. I have been through the baptism in the Holy Spirit. I pray every day. At a retreat last year we were asked "how do we let God love us?" I pondered this question because I did not have an immediate answer. That night I went to bed and prayed to the Father, "How do I let You in? I don't even know if I do." And I lay in bed and said, "Lord, I don't even know how to answer that question, please help me." As I lay there the Lord said, "You don't let me in." And I just broke down. I said, "Well, what am I doing?" And He said, "You're just so performance-based. It's not about the number of prayers you say, how often you go to Mass. It's not about that. It's about getting to know Me and letting your guard down for Me. Which is why you have no intimacy in your life. You don't let people in."

Intimacy's been a very hard thing for me, and as I study your material I realize I'm gripped by pride and I'm gripped by some of the sinful things I've done in my life. I was a good kid growing up. I mean, I didn't drink and I didn't smoke and I had a girlfriend all through high school and two years of college, and I was never sexually intimate with her. Not that we didn't embrace and kiss and stuff, but I was a good guy. And when I stopped being a good guy I got really bad.

And so one day prior to Easter—I was about twenty-six—I went to confession and the priest refused to give me absolution. In front of literally a hundred and some people in the church, he chased me out of the confessional. It was really a stunning experience.

Neal: *Were you going to confession regularly before that?*

S: Yeah, pretty much.

Neal: *To this priest?*

S: No. He didn't know me and I didn't know him. And the good part of it was I think the Lord protected me because I was in a church where nobody knew me, and I thought oh my gosh, that's a blessing unto itself. If I had been in my hometown, it would have been devastating [nervous laughter]. I would have had to move, go into a witness protection program. But I had a very horrific experience. I was single, and I went to a singles place one night, took a young lady home, and about a month later she called and said she was pregnant. She wanted money to get an abortion, and quite honestly I was so frightened I just met her in a parking lot and gave her the money to "fix" the situation. And whether she was pregnant or not—I have always believed that she was—I had sex with her. In my travels I learned about Rachel's Vineyard. I did a Rachel's Vineyard weekend where you named the child and learned of God's infinite mercy. I feel one of the things that has happened as a result of your conference is that all of my sins are being revealed to me, almost as if it were yesterday. It's overwhelming.

NEAL: *Can we start with when you turned from being the good guy to the bad guy, as you call it?*

S: Yeah, it was after college. I was probably twenty-two years old. A group of guys got a house on the Eastern Shore of Maryland in the summertime. There wasn't a whole lot of sacramental grace flowing around this atmosphere. And the thing that I think is really at the crux of my issues is that when I was a young boy, my father was an inordinately angry man. The littlest thing could set him off. Everything was wrong, and it was wrong every day. He had an awful temper. And I do believe that aggression begets aggression. I saw it in myself as a young boy. I was fearless. I would look for opportunities to show how fearless I was, even though I was a skinny little kid. If someone made fun of me, I could defend myself at the drop of a dime.

So there was a lot of anxiety in our house—a lot of anger and a lot of shouting. When I was nine my dad got sick and lost his business in Newark, Delaware, and we moved down to the country where he found work, but he got even angrier because he felt he had failed. So that year, because I had been in a parochial school, I was ahead of the kids in public school, but there was so much anxiety [in me] between the different schools and the new neighborhood, and the anxiety had accelerated because of my father's illness and his losing the business. And one day I got called down to the principal's office because I was rocking in my seat. This is something that's become really clear to me recently. I was rocking because it felt good and it led to making an even more interesting discovery: that there could be other ways to feel good rather than just rocking.

NEAL: *This is third grade?*

S: I was nine years old, and I began masturbating and it overwhelmed me, it consumed my life. I remember in college I would go down into the stacks below the library where no one would see me or find me, and I would find any magazine that might have a picture to stimulate me. Masturbation became my anxiety release, and I did it as often as I could. Afterwards, I would become angry with myself for my sinfulness and turn to a priest for healing and confession. It was a long journey for me, and I never connected the reason that I was finding a way to satisfy myself during stress and anxiety and in the process crushing my self-esteem with self-loathing and self-condemnation. I did not realize that I had developed an addiction of self-abuse. I've always feared an absence of God in my life, but I did not trust in Him enough to find a real cure for my addiction. I went four years without going to a Catholic church after that negative incident, but I did go to church on Sundays.

NEAL: *After what incident, that confession?*

S: Yes. Then I went several years without going to a Catholic church, but I would go someplace on Sunday. Then I went to hear a speaker at our Catholic church in the city where I was living near the Eastern Shore. I went because they were featuring this exciting speaker and confession afterwards, and I felt this would be a great time for me to confess my abortion involvement and absence of absolution from my last confession. I felt, wow, you know? It'd been three or four years, the longest time I'd ever been without going to confession since I was probably six years old.

So that night this priest, a wonderful guy, asked me after my confession if I believed my sins were forgiven, and I said "I hope so." He said, "That wasn't the question I asked you. Do you believe God in Scripture who says if you have remorse and truly seek absolution for your sins, God will not remember your sins from as far as the east is from the west? He is all-merciful. Pray to overcome your addiction, and pray for a good woman to come into your life." The next Sunday I began going to Mass and communion faithfully, and I began to say prayers to find that "good" woman and removed myself from situations where I would be in temptation. Two years later I met my wife. It was through this holy priest that I understood God would forgive me but that I also had to learn to forgive myself. But my years of turning inward to satisfy myself became my new cross, because whenever anxiety presented itself I would return to the solution engrained in me since I was nine years old, and this affected my relationships, especially with my wife. So I began to pray to have that intimacy that she so deserved and I desired to provide for her.

Throughout all my struggles my saving grace has been the priesthood. I never committed the sin of self-abuse with the notion that I could run to a priest and confess it and it was all okay. The sexual trigger that fed my addiction was everywhere. It would come on me with such force I was unable to shut it down. After completing the act, I was so despondent I would seek out a priest. I confessed but never really got into an intimate "Father, please help me…" kind of dialogue.

NEAL: *How many children do you have?*

S: I have five children. I've been married now twenty years, and I just celebrated my fifty-fifth birthday.

NEAL: *Let's focus on your stuff that we have to deal with today, okay? So after college you were involved in drinking, partying…*

S: Not a heavy drinker, but I drank beyond my limits way too often. I thought I should be able to drink like the other guys, but alcohol was toxic to my system. I thought everyone got hangovers and it was normal. I didn't realize at the time that hangovers mean you're poisoning your system. I wish I had known that at a younger age. I believe I could have prevented many unfortunate encounters. Alcohol, however, was just another escape, and it was better than the pain I experienced, so I was not looking for a solution. It wasn't until I got married with young children that I realized the Lord was calling me to tackle yet another weakness.

NEAL: *When you said it got really dark, what do you mean?*

S: Sexually. I was just way, way too overactive post-college, pre-marriage, and there was no shortage of willing partners during those dark days. Looking back I realize that I was a physically selfish human being.

I would have been really attracted to a woman that was different, someone who held herself out as special.

NEAL: *Can you clarify that?*

S: I was monogamous in my activity; I didn't have multiple partners and I didn't do drugs. But I would find someone that I was very attracted to and we would get intimately involved, and I didn't understand that I was tampering with this young woman's emotional well-being. I thought she approached sex the same way I did. Now I am so sad not to have been a spiritual beacon for every woman I met. I mean, I pray for those women who were in my life, and I try to say, well, it takes two; you didn't force anyone to bed down with you. Was this Satan whispering in my ear? I wasn't a holy man; I wasn't a righteous man whatsoever.

NEAL: *So what's the biggest thing you're carrying, the guilt?*

S: The abortion, the lack of intimacy, and I was able ultimately to connect with the self-abuse and what that was doing to my life, but it took a toll on my life for way too long.

NEAL: *Did you start looking at pornography?*

S: I did, and ultimately what I ended up doing is taking pictures of Jesus and putting them everywhere—over computers, every place I could. I was trying not to be overwhelmed, because I think I had patterned my brain. I've read a lot of stuff about that, and I think I patterned my brain to the point where if I had the slightest provocation, the rush became overwhelming. I reached the point where I got really scared that I had destroyed my ability to control my conscious mind, and my subconscious was in total control, and I was now on sexual image auto-pilot. Picture, rush, release. Then regret and humiliation for my lack of discipline followed by self-loathing. The least bit of stress or anxiety with provocative stimulation and the cycle repeated itself over and over. I began praying and trying to understand the actual initial provocation so that my life wasn't totally out of control, but it didn't always work and I found myself out of touch with my true feelings.

NEAL: *And how are you getting along with your wife?*

S: Good, but I'm not what I should be, and your Unbound conference on deliverance was an epiphany for me. I want to be able to give her all my love.

Neal: *And to receive her love?*

S: And to allow her to love me. I think for most of my life my difficulties have been self-inflicted, except for my mother, who just loved me unconditionally. I am blessed that she was there so that I know what it's like. But I think because of the fear of conflict in the house and finding ways to make myself feel good in an environment of anxiety I never learned how to love myself. As a result, I didn't know how to let others into the space that I didn't allow myself to go. I think things, they've attached to me that I am yet to release. This became abundantly clear in your conference; I realized the Lord was not done with my need for purification. When you were speaking I knew that you knew my heart though we had never met.

Neal: *Is there anything else you want to share about your dad and your particular situation?*

S: While he never gave me a personal blessing, I believe he left me with a spiritual memory. He was devout in his faith and to the Church. He was a Grand Knight and District Deputy in the Knights of Columbus, and often I saw him saying his rosary kneeling beside his bed. I really believe that he did the best he knew how or he would have done better. Unfortunately, his blistering temper caused a lot of tension and strife for me and my siblings. In my readings I learned that healing comes from forgiveness. In no way did I want to forgive my dad. On the other hand, I did not want to live a life of bitterness. I desperately wanted a better life, so I discussed it with my mom, who encouraged me to step out in faith and confront my dad. I was petrified. No one confronted my dad, but I believe the Holy Spirit protected me because he was completely taken off guard when I said, "Dad, there is something I need to tell you. Is this a good time?" "What is it?" he said. "Well, I've been meaning to tell you how much I know you sacrifice for all of us, and I just wanted to tell you I love you. Since you've never told me you loved me I thought I would break the ice." (I was twenty-one years old.)

I could tell he was nervous and felt guilty and didn't know what to say. The good news was he didn't hit me. "What got into you?" he said. "What are they teaching you at that school?" (I was a junior in college.) I said, "Dad, you must desire to have a relationship with your son, as much as I want to have one with my father. What's in the way?" "Nothing," he said, "you know I love you." "Only because Mom tells me you do, but I thought just once it would be nice to hear it from you." Then he said the magic words: "I don't know why I don't tell you, but I do love you." From that day forward everything was different, not great but better. Unfortunately, my anxiety addiction was not cured. Meanwhile my siblings, who never reconciled their relationship with Dad, were angry with me several years later when he died. When he was dying, I would drive two hours every night after work and spend the night at his bedside. We had our own time together for probably five or six years before he died, and I forgave him for being an unhealthy, mean-spirited role model. I mean I didn't have to write a letter and take it to his grave; I forgave him years before. My siblings did not know that Dad and I had those conversations years before. When they found out they were angry I had not shared my experience. They never received a father's blessing. And while I had the opportunity to reconcile my relationship, they hungered for an opportunity lost.

While I struggled with trying to understand my siblings' attitude toward me, it wasn't until I was sitting in your UNBOUND seminar that I understood that temptation was not just a struggle against personal weaknesses but was in fact a strategic, demonic campaign to derail me and to destroy my faith. I understood that I still had a spirit attachment which prevented me from crying out for the Father's daily blessing. I realized that Satan wanted me to be focused on the obstacles in my life to prevent me from receiving, in Christ, the Father's blessing.

I never understood that the damage done could be renounced and for all those that I harmed, I could ask the Father to forgive me, and for all those who harmed me, I could, in the Father's name, forgive. This was the message I had been looking for. I had done a lot on my own, but I had never forgiven myself; Satan still had me in bondage. So my siblings never forgave me for not sharing with them the experience I had with Dad. And I said to them it never occurred to me.

I had my own pain I was trying to work on. Deep down the reason I never shared my experience is because they were very cynical and I did not want to be made fun of by sharing my feelings. Everyone has their own relationship with their parents; I did what I needed to do at the time. It would almost have been like boasting, like "look what I'm doing." It never occurred to me to do that.

NEAL: *And they said?*

S: We wish we had done that but you should have told us.

NEAL: *What do you mean they didn't do what you did?*

S: They never had that conversation with Dad. I still find their cynicism toxic; it is too much a reminder of my childhood, so I choose to have a cordial long-distance relationship. I am trying to find a way to forgive my uncle who lived next door to us and was my brother's age and his best friend. When I was fourteen years old my brother who was eighteen and his friend went on a camping trip, and we shared a large cabin together. My brother and his friend were my idols; I thought they were everything I wasn't. Off the charts. Super bright, talented, lots of friends. That night on the camping trip, my brother's friend reached over and touched me. I was a tough little kid, but I was afraid to call him out.

NEAL: *What name can I use to refer to your brother's friend in prayer?*

S: Call him H. The next morning I told my brother what happened and he said no way, I must be mistaken. The shock of that experience really never left me. The conflict of that was it's bad enough not having a father's blessing, but to have the next male in your family fail to protect your innocence was crushing. Years later after my mother and father died, my brother and his childhood best friend came out of the closet and became an item. I believed my brother knew from the beginning and perhaps he used his friend to test me. It destroyed our relationship to this day. I will attempt to take what I learn here at UNBOUND to find a way to forgive him. This will not be easy, but I want to be completely healed. My brother became a very in-your-face homosexual. A conversation with him was about his gay barber, his gay mechanic, and I'm like "yeah, right, give it up, I don't talk about my..."

NEAL: *Heterosexual...*

S: Exactly, my heterosexual mechanic, my heterosexual barber. It's a terrible irritant. And my other siblings think he...I mean, they don't know that, and I would never...

NEAL: *They don't know he's homosexual?*

S: Oh yeah, but they never knew about him not protecting me when I was abused, and how I believe he knew all along that his friend was gay and just testing me.

NEAL: *His friend touching you?*

S: Yeah. Nor would I ever, but they just love him and think he's real special and that's good for him, but it's a real trial for me because I'd love to spill the beans, but I believe I'm called not to do that.

NEAL: *Okay, any other major things that happened to you that you want to cover today?*

S: When I had moved into this new town, there was a group of boys, three or four, that I became friendly with, and one young boy who was really admired by a lot of the kids—he molested me.

NEAL: *How old were you?*

S: Probably twelve, thirteen. We were sleeping out one night in a tent, an ugly moment.

NEAL: *Do you remember his first name?*

S: G.

NEAL: *Did he actually...?*

S: Oh, he entered me and...

NEAL: *Okay.*

S: I was just...

Neal: *And you didn't fight him because you were…*

S: Initially, I just knew that this was wrong. I was intimidated.

Neal: *Okay, and you'd been masturbating for a couple of years?*

S: By that time. From the time I was about nine years old.

Neal: *Those are two real good things to cover today. You mentioned you were performance-based. Did you mention the word pride?*

S: Oh yeah. And a fear of rejection. As I was reading your book, I could trace this back to early rejection that's been attached to me all my life. And I think the sister to that is the fear of offense, I was so easily offended. Still am, but if my worst was 10, I'm a 1 or 2 now. I became aware of this about two years ago and I really prayed and worked hard on not allowing myself to get offended and hurt so easily. I believe a big part of it was recognizing it, and I think I'm coming out the other end. I'm trying to do the same with the fear of rejection.

Neal: *Could you explain the fear of offense? Is it the fear of somebody saying something mean to you or hurting you, is that what it means?*

S: That's part of it, but I believe it's mostly people not agreeing with my point of view. I'm not accepting of other people's point of view when I perceive it to be different from my own.

Neal: *And your emotional reaction to something like that is what? Is it hurt or anger or both?*

S: No, hurt.

Neal: *Hurt.*

S: Yes, not anger.

Neal: *Okay.*

S: Two days ago a business guy called me and I got back to him the next day and he said, "I called you yesterday. Things must be really good that you couldn't get back to me." It was like, wow, there it is—it's coming after me again. But at least I was aware of it, I knew to apologize to him rather than…normally I would have defended it. And I know I'm healing in this area because I said: "I should have gotten back to you yesterday, I'm sorry I didn't," and I just left it there. For all my adult life I would never have been able to do that.

NEAL: *So you always defend yourself?*

S: Always.

NEAL: *That's called self-justification.*

S: Right.

NEAL: *And that's a big issue.*

S: I could be in the whole thing for that.

NEAL: *You see, you know your stuff. That's great.*

S: And I'm learning from you. That's why I'm grateful that you would see me today because you touched me, very special. You're what I needed that day. I knew it. And nobody ever reached me the way you did. I'm so grateful I met you, it was just that simple.

NEAL: *All right, the pride goes along with self-justification, self-righteousness. And are you stubborn?*

S: I've been told that, and while I don't apply that moniker to myself, I know I am strong-willed.

NEAL: *Okay, and then sometimes those things lead to things like judgment of others.*

S: I have a pet phrase that I say when I sin with my eyes. I started about a year ago. I'd say to the Lord, "I'd be better blind, I wouldn't sin as much. That's not a request, please. I want You to know that I need You to somehow cover my sight that's causing me to judge others." The hardest for me is sexual immodesty, it's a trigger for me and it's everywhere. I've trained myself to focus on the other person's eyes to avoid drifting into temptation. Because of my own insecurities I could find something wrong with just about anyone: purple hair, wires connected from their nose to their ear, tattoos, or whatever. I tried to see what our Creator sees in these people, or just let me see something else, let me find out why it is that they're so special in His eyes. So I say a little prayer in the morning to let me see the Christ in others; where there's potential in me to show that, let it reveal itself. It's been very helpful. He's been like my own personal coach. I have to do it every day or I begin to fall into old patterns.

NEAL: *Good. So other things that go with that are judgment, condemnation, criticism, comparison. I wanted to ask you do you have a fear of intimacy, do you think that's a way of describing it, or is it just a lack of enthusiasm?*

S: No, I think I have a fear of intimacy. I think if that were to occur I wouldn't know who I am. I have such a protective insecure identity; I don't know what that new identity would look like.

NEAL: *Just a couple more things here. I wrote down self-protection, does that make sense? And going along with the pride—independence.*

S: Very much so.

NEAL: *Self-reliance.*

S: Very much so.

NEAL: *How about isolation?*

S: I can deal with that. I have lots of interests and can easily occupy my time.

NEAL: *Do you struggle with loneliness?*

S: I don't have loneliness.

NEAL: *That's good. Anything else you'd like to cover? Let me go over what I wrote. You don't need to forgive your mom. You did forgive your dad. We'll just say a quick word of forgiveness toward your mother and your dad. Your dad you forgave and it's really deep, it's obvious, but we'll just say a couple of things to see if it will go deeper, okay?*

S: Sure.

NEAL: *You want to forgive your brother.*

S: I do.

Neal: *Okay, we pronounce forgiveness of that. And I can lead you to forgive the priest in the confessional.*

S: I do.

Neal: *So you've been working on all that; we just want to make sure that's covered as we move along. I wrote down self-hatred, self-condemnation, self-rejection, self-abuse, and fear of rejection, fear of abandonment, spirit of rejection, and spirit of abandonment.*

S: Not so much the abandonment as it is the spirit of offense.

Neal: *The fear of offense?*

S: Yes.

Neal: *Did you ever feel like an orphan or fatherless?*

S: I never had that feeling.

Neal: *Okay. Because sometimes [when] the father is an orphan that carries on, and more than anything what happens is they don't bond, they don't know how to bond and there's rejection.*

S: You know, Neal, it could be there and I don't recognize it.

Neal: *No, you would have had thoughts probably. If you want to renounce it you can, but often people have thoughts of "maybe I'm adopted…"*

S: My brother and sister used to tell me I was adopted, but I always thought that was funny.

Neal: *If you were under an orphan spirit you wouldn't have thought it was funny. You would have been hurt or been suspicious. So it's unlikely but certainly the rejection is there. I wrote down anger, resentment, bitterness, retaliation, revenge, violence.*

S: There was a time in my life when I was younger that they were all on display. I've worked on lots of them but never knew why I still have an absence of joy.

Neal: *You mentioned the violence when you were young.*

S: Yeah, I loved to fight, it's just like…

Neal: *So even though it's years ago, it's good to cover it.*

S: Okay.

Neal: *And with that sometimes comes hatred. Did you experience hatred back then?*

S: No question.

Neal: *Did you ever have a desire to kill someone or fantasize about killing?*

S: No.

Neal: *I wrote down anxiety, fear, fear of intimacy.*

S: I will say this though, I never had a fear of taking someone else's life but I had a fear of taking my own. More than once.

Neal: *You mean you had the thought come to your mind?*

S: I did. A priest in confession said it was the spirit of murder. I prayed to be free of that.

Neal: *Spirit of suicide, death, and also escape.*

S: Oh yeah.

Neal: *And sometimes with that is hiding.*

S: Yup.

Neal: *So hiding and escape can build into alcoholism or it can build into stuff like suicide.*

S: My father was an alcoholic. I don't remember him drinking when I was young; it seemed to come later in life, probably sometime in his fifties. The alcohol gene is alive and well for most segments of my ancestry and my family, but somehow I'm protected from that gene. There have been times I wished I wasn't [laughter] but I can't tolerate alcohol.

Neal: *The escape and hiding from the experience in your family led into the masturbation. Do you struggle with masturbation now? Did you ever struggle with masturbation since you were married?*

S: Yes, I did. I struggled with masturbation up until probably five or six years ago. I have such enormous regret about time wasted and my sinfulness, it's pretty overwhelming.

NEAL: *And is that guilt?*

S: Oh, yeah.

NEAL: *Regret. Any other name you'd put to that? Regret and self-loathing?*

S: You know, I think of who I could have been, the gifts that He gave me...

NEAL: *Let me share this with you. I was just about to share with you about pride, self-justification, self-righteousness, stubbornness, judgment, criticism, comparison, condemnation...that's a basis for you to know what you've been given.*

S: I do.

NEAL: *So the issue is really forgiving yourself.*

S: Amen.

NEAL: *And those things are rooted and binding you, they limit your ability to forgive yourself. The regrets and the guilt.*

S: Yes, and the reason I needed to come back to see you was that at the conference nothing happened to me and I was like on the K list, which they didn't get to, and I thought maybe that's part of God's plan because it opened the door to have a personal conference with you, and then I went up to where you were standing at the end of the conference and you were doing the blessing, and you laid hands on me and said: "Even though you didn't have your father's blessing, your heavenly Father blesses you and is calling you." I was stunned by your prophecy, it was true: I didn't have my father's blessing growing up and would never have received it as a young adult if I hadn't asked for it. I said to you, "How did you know that?" You said in effect it was not something you knew, it was something revealed to you. I knew the Holy Spirit was present and wanted me to experience deliverance. The next morning there was a feeling in me that I had never felt before. It was...I can't describe it,

I just felt alive and I knew something had happened at that healing. I felt a new confidence to reach out to my heavenly Father with praise and joy. I just wanted to take it deeper and further.

NEAL: *Well, we've got more time today. So the rest I have written down is lust and pornography, fornication, spirit that entered through pornography, and breaking soul ties, and we'll just cover these things and see what God does, all right?*

S: And at the top of that list is to repent from my sins, the absence of intimacy, just to be able to be intimate—that would be such a blessing in my life.

NEAL: *All right.*

Lord, I want to thank You for S, I thank You for his life and this journey he's been on and all the ways Your grace has been at work in him. We ask You, Lord, to take him to a new level of freedom today. Break the power of all these lies he's been living under. I thank You, Lord.

Just repeat after me, and if I say something that's not quite right, you can just change it, all right? Say,

NEAL SPEAKS AND S REPEATS:

Lord Jesus. I thank You for dying for my sins and defeating my enemies. Thank You that I can choose today to live under Your freedom, to break the hold the enemy has. I ask You, Lord, to receive me, I ask You to give me your Holy Spirit; Lord, I will follow You. Lord, thank You for Your mercy and Your kindness. I ask You to forgive me for withholding my heart from my wife and my children, and I ask You to set me free from the fear of intimacy. **KEY 1**

In the name of Jesus I forgive my mom for not protecting me from my dad's wrath and his criticism and his anger. I forgive her for not helping me to understand what was going on; I forgive her for not knowing my heart and helping me to understand. In the name of Jesus, I forgive my dad for his anger, for every day thinking something was wrong, for his criticism, for the anxiety he caused me. I forgive him for not being the father I needed him to be, I forgive him for not spending time with me and letting me know I was special. In the name of Jesus

I forgive him for not blessing my manhood and showing me what it means to be a man. I forgive him for not helping me to understand my body when I began to masturbate. I forgive him for not protecting me from my brother's friend who touched me and G who molested me. I forgive him in the name of Jesus. In the name of Jesus, I forgive my brother for the day he refused to believe me and caused me anxiety, humiliation, and confusion. I forgive him in the name of Jesus. In the name of Jesus, I forgive my brother's friend H for touching me and causing me anxiety, humiliation, and confusion. In the name of Jesus, I forgive G for betraying my friendship and leading me into sin. I forgive him for touching me, penetrating me; I forgive him in the name of Jesus. In the name of Jesus, I forgive the priest that said my soul was so black he would not give me absolution. I forgive him for humiliating me, chasing me out of the confessional. Lord, have mercy on his soul. In the name of Jesus, I forgive myself for all my sins, for all my sexual sins, for all the women that I used. In the name of Jesus, I forgive myself for the lack of intimacy, for withholding my heart from my wife. I forgive myself for always needing to do it myself, for not showing my weakness and letting others help me, especially You, Lord. **KEY 2**

In the name of Jesus, I renounce every physical and spiritual tie with E (He filled in the name of one of the women he had sexual intercourse with) and I take back what I gave to her. (This was repeated giving him the opportunity to fill in the first name or in some way identify other women he had been with.) In the name of Jesus, I renounce every physical and spiritual tie with G, and I take back what I gave to him, and I take back what he took from me. In the name of Jesus, I renounce every physical and spiritual tie with that woman who claimed to be pregnant and had an abortion, and I take back what I gave to her. In the name of Jesus, I break the power of any spirit that came to me through that encounter. In the name of Jesus, I renounce the spirit of abortion. In the name of Jesus, I renounce the spirit of death. In the name of Jesus, I renounce every physical and spiritual tie with D, and I take back what I gave to her. [Repeated for other women.] In the name of Jesus Christ, I break the power of every physical and spiritual tie of with every woman that I fornicated with, and I take back what I gave to them and I reserve myself for my beautiful wife. In the name of Jesus, I renounce the fear of intimacy. [Repeated for] self-rejection, self-hatred, self-condemnation, a spirit of masturbation, self-abuse, spirit of rejection, fear of rejection, fear of offense, spirit of hurt, retaliation, anger, resentment, bitterness, spirit of rage, violence, hatred, anxiety, fear, spirit of self-protection, independence, self-reliance, isolation, pride, self-justification, self-righteousness, stubbornness, fear of being wrong, spirit of judgment, condemnation, self-condemnation, fear of condemnation, criticism, fear of criticism, lust, pornography, and any spirit that entered me when I watched it and any spirit that's operating in that physical reaction, I renounce that spirit, spirit of fornication, spirit of regret, guilt, suicide, spirit of escape, spirit of hiding.

NEAL: *Anything else you want to renounce?*

S: I want to renounce any behavior toward my children that may have caused them to have anxiety, fear, or anger.

NEAL SPEAKS AND S REPEATS: Lord Jesus, in the name of Jesus, I forgive myself for not emotionally supporting my children better and not making better decisions. In the name of Jesus, I forgive myself for every stupid decision I ever made. In the name of Jesus, I renounce the spirit of homelessness and the spirit of being lost. (Note: I felt led to lead him this way based on his lifelong expressions of repentance and the issues of pride that often indicate the deeper bondage is in failing to forgive oneself.)

NEAL: *Now just be quiet. I don't want you to pray, I just want you to capture any thought that comes to your mind, okay?*

In the name of Jesus Christ, I break the power of every spirit you have renounced and I command them to leave right now in Jesus' name.

(Moment of silence.) *What's coming to you?*

S: I have a sense of being at the Father's table with many saints.

NEAL SPEAKS AND S REPEATS: Thank You, Lord, that I'm a member of Your family, that I belong and I'm safe. That I can be myself. Thank You, Lord, that I am loved. I am free to be loved.

Neal: *How do you feel when you say that?*

S: I feel wonderful.

Neal: *Amen.*

S: Amen.

Neal: *I want you to stand up. We're going to pray a blessing on you.*

Thank You, Father. Thank You, Lord. Father, I thank You that S sees himself at table with you, he is part of Your family and he has a right to be there. Jesus has made him worthy, he belongs.

I declare that the Lord has taken your sins as far as the east is from the west, and He sees them no more. I declare you are free not to hold them anymore, not to say "this is who I am." You are free not to continue in sin. This is not who you are. You have been baptized into Christ, your sins have been taken, His blood has washed you, and you are a new creation. Your old identity is gone, your new identity has come, you are in Christ Jesus. As you sit at table with the Father, it is Jesus the eternal Son who dwells in you, He shines through you. The Father's delight in you is the same delight He has in His Son. I speak blessing over you and declare that at the moment you were conceived the Father blessed you, and on the day you were born He opened up heaven and said "This is My son, My beloved son in whom I take great delight. This is My son…this is My son…this is My son."

I ask that the blessing of the Father would be released upon you. I ask that the blessing that was robbed from S's father when his father died would be restored to S and that he would be able to bless His children and wife from the place of having received, knowing he is loved, knowing he is forgiven, and that mercy and forgiveness would flow through him to everyone in his life, and that it would be a testimony that the man who has suffered has overcome by the blood of the Lamb. **KEY 5**

Appendix B

DESCRIPTION OF MINISTRY DOCUMENTS
AND TOOLS FOUND IN APPENDIX B

PART 1. PRAYER MINISTRY TRAINING OUTLINE: This article can be used as a handout for those being trained and as an outline for a presentation preparing teams for UNBOUND ministry.

PART 2. LEARNING TO LISTEN: Use this note-taking form to help you note what the Lord uncovers in an interview. An alternate note-taking form can be found on our website.

PART 3. DISCERNMENT: This article discusses discernment and its use in the model of deliverance in UNBOUND MINISTRY. It is not intended to be complete in itself. Reading *UNBOUND: A Practical Guide to Deliverance*, attending an UNBOUND conference, and/or listening to the conference CDs is recommended.

PART 4. SAMPLES OF RELATED SPIRITS: This is a list of evil spirits that can often be related and is helpful when listening to a person's story. These spirits often—but not always—go together.

PART 5. LIES TO RENOUNCE: This document gives you examples of the range of lies that may be uncovered in a ministry session. The lies are as unique as the person's story. Reflecting on this list will help you listen for particular lies as they are expressed. As with the Samples of Related Spirits, this document is not meant to be memorized but rather to be used as an informative reference.

PART 6. DEVELOPING AN UNBOUND MINISTRY: Members of one church started an UNBOUND prayer ministry team after helping host a conference at their church in March of 2009. Read on to find out how they approached developing an UNBOUND team. Their experience is very valuable and may help you adapt the principles of UNBOUND to prayer ministry in your own church or group.

Appendix B

Part 1: Prayer Ministry Training Outline

OVERALL TRAINING OBJECTIVE: To ensure prayer ministry team members have the necessary attitude, information, and experience to effectively lead ministry using the Five Keys of the UNBOUND model.

To prepare both prayer leaders and intercessors for ministry.

PRAYER MINISTRY MEASURE OF SUCCESS

PRIMARY: That the person receiving prayer felt loved, accepted, and listened to.

SECONDARY: That the person was led faithfully through the Five Keys without being given advice or other forms of counseling.

Prayer team is **not** responsible for freedom—this is the Lord's work.

NOTE: As the primary measure of success in prayer ministry is that the person feels loved, accepted, and listened to, it is not essential that prayer leaders have extensive training and experience. However, it is important that leaders are familiar with the model and are comfortable and confident so as they step out in faith, the Lord will be able to use them in His service.

PRAYER MINISTRY TEAM MEMBER CHECKLIST: Prior to being on a ministry team, individuals must have:

- A personal relationship with the Lord and seriousness about their own spiritual journey.
- Read *UNBOUND* and ideally have attended an UNBOUND conference (live or via CD or DVD).
- Received leadership training in use of the Five Keys.
- Familiarity with related spirits and entryways.
- Participated in a prayer ministry session as an observer (i.e., intercessor) one or more times.
- Discretion and respect for confidentiality.

- Willingness to use *only* the UNBOUND model during the prayer ministry session.
- Received prayer ministry using the Five Keys (ideally—this is not mandatory).
- Confidence in the Holy Spirit to lead.
- Freedom from expectations that the person **must** be free by end of session; realization that the process of gaining freedom is ongoing.
- Ability to love the person where they are at without judgment—and to listen in light of the Five Keys.

How Team Members Can Prepare for Ministry:

- Review the Five Keys, related spirits, etc.
- Draw near to the Lord and rely on Him
- Admit any fears and pride
- Confess your sins
- Intercede for the team and person receiving prayer
- Ask the Holy Spirit to lead the person receiving prayer and the ministry team

Outline of a Ministry Session:

- Prepare the environment
- Warmly welcome the person
- All women's teams can pray **only** with women. Similar for teams of all men.
- Explain/clarify the process; explain confidentiality and that notes will be destroyed; role of intercessor
- Freedom is a journey; additional opportunities exist after current ministry session

- Start with a prayer (keep it simple)
- Listen to the story. Ask questions as appropriate (think about the entryways; look for patterns and connections between spirits)
- Listen to the Holy Spirit (avoid being mechanical in the process)
- Do not try too hard or go where you're not clearly welcome
- Be mindful of your posture (you may pull closer or take their hand when you start to lead them through the keys; always ask before touching someone; stand for the blessing)
- Have confidence in God, not in your papers
- **Keep your eyes open** — observe what's going on
- Make notes regarding the Five Keys (possibly using a note-taking tool)
- Validate notes with the person and confirm related spirits
- Don't have them renounce everything on the page of sample spirits — only what applies to their story
- Lead prayer through the Five Keys

    KEY 1 Repentance and faith

    KEY 2 Forgiveness

    KEY 3 Renunciation

    KEY 4 Authority (Thanksgiving to confirm/test for freedom)

    KEY 5 Father's blessing

- It's perfectly okay to go back to the interview if something new comes up
- Ask if they have any questions and provide an overview of next steps (e.g., community support, using the Five Keys yourself, awareness of having moved from a place of bondage to a place of weakness, value of journaling and recording personal enemies) and ask if a follow-up email would be okay

- ✣ Do **not** provide counseling or advice. Avoid using the phrase "you should…"
- ✣ Do **not** tell the person he/she is free. It is his/her story and he/she is the one to tell it.

Some Tips for Ministry:

- ✣ Remember that freedom is about our identity, life's purpose, and destiny in Christ; about being beloved sons and daughters of God, with a future full of hope, and an eternal destiny of everlasting life, sharing in His inheritance
- ✣ Listen for the Five Keys (use one of the interview tools)—don't get caught up in details
- ✣ Listen without judgment or shock at what is heard
- ✣ Listen like a coach (encouraging, supportive—looking forward to what the Lord will do), but not with pity (or emotional attachment or focusing on the past or on the pain)
- ✣ Instead of asking "why," ask "Have you always felt this way?" or "When did you start to feel this way?"
- ✣ Pay attention to potential "identity" issues (e.g., "I am a victim"; "I am helpless"; "I am lost"; "I am worthless")

Ministry Resources (partial list):

- ✣ *Unbound: A Practical Guide to Deliverance*
- ✣ *Unbound Ministry Guidebook*
- ✣ *Resisting the Devil*
- ✣ *Unbound: Freedom in Christ Companion Guide*
- ✣ List of entryways (e.g., unrepented or habitual sin, relationships, trauma, occult, agreement with lies/curses, generational)
- ✣ List of related spirits

Appendix B

- List of sample lies
- Interview/note-taking tools (various formats)

Part 2: Learning to Listen Practice Sheet

REPENTANCE AND FAITH *Lord please forgive me for... Lord I am sorry for... Thank you for... I surrender... please... (Commitment to Christ)* — **KEY 1**

_____
_____
_____

KEY POINTS OF THE STORY

_____
_____
_____
_____

ENEMIES TO RENOUNCE

_____
_____
_____
_____
_____
_____
_____
_____
_____
_____
_____

RELATED SPIRITS

_____
_____
_____
_____
_____
_____
_____
_____
_____
_____
_____

PEOPLE TO FORGIVE — **KEY 2**
In the name of Jesus I forgive_____ for _____. (be specific)

_____
_____
_____

KEY 3

OCCULT *In the name of Jesus... I renounce the (any) spirit that came to me when... I renounce the spirit that operated in _____ (i.e. fortune teller, etc.) and I take back the Authority (power) I gave to _____ (name).*

_____
_____

SOUL TIES *I renounce every unholy tie with... I renounce every physical and spiritual tie with_____ and I take back the authority I gave to him/her (or what he/she took from me).*

_____

KEY 4 — **COMMAND** *In the name of Jesus I break the power of every spirit that _____ has renounced, and I command it to go right now.*

THANKSGIVING *and declarations of faith related to repentance, forgiveness, and renunciation...*

KEY 5 — **THE FATHER'S BLESSING AND FOLLOW-UP INSTRUCTIONS**

Appendix B

Part 3: Discernment:

DISCERNMENT OF SPIRITS

To one there is given through the Spirit a message of wisdom, to another a message of knowledge by means of the same Spirit, to another faith by the same Spirit, to another gifts of healing by that one Spirit, to another miraculous powers, to another prophecy, to another distinguishing between spirits, to another speaking in different kinds of tongues, and to still another the interpretation of tongues.

1 Corinthians 12:8-10 (NIV)

Discernment is a gift from the Lord. By this gift, God enables us to understand the motives of one's heart and to recognize where an action comes from. Is it from the Spirit of God, the human spirit, or an evil spirit? Does it flow from truth or a lie?

Since it is a gift of the Holy Spirit, we need to continually rely on the Lord to lead us and not operate simply on our own knowledge. As with any gift, discernment is not isolated from knowledge. The gift develops in the context of reflection, study, and experience. Whether we have a strong spiritual gift or small gift of discernment, we can learn to be more effective in using the gift we have been given.

The context of discernment must be love and humble service. The gift of discernment used by immature or wounded individuals may become a means of self-protection or control. Under a spirit of self-deception, one may disguise judgment, criticism, gossip, and even slander as the gift of discernment. It can be a weapon: "You are filled with pride." "You need deliverance." "You need to renounce rebellion." "She has a spirit of division." "He has a spirit of envy." "You have a controlling spirit." Statements like these can cause great harm. Anyone seeking to grow in the gift of discernment should be aware of these dangers. The best preparation for using the gift of discernment is self-knowledge. The Holy Spirit brings us through a process of brokenness in which God reveals to us our hearts. The first book I wrote was *The Older Brother Returns*. This is my story of how God exposed my heart and what I learned from it. Being aware of our own weakness enables us to serve another humbly.

Spirits Are Related

In the interview process we use in the UNBOUND model of deliverance, spirits, lies, and/or bindings are revealed. We are aware spirits work together as a means of hiding the root entryway or root spirit, deepening their binding of the person, and building a pattern of thinking that is a stronghold. It is helpful to become aware of typical groupings of spirits. For example: anger, rage, hatred, revenge, retaliation, bitterness, resentment, violence, murder, unforgiveness… Consider how these spirits are interrelated. Think about how similar and different they are. We cannot name and gain authority over hatred by calling it anger. We cannot have victory over a spirit of violence if we do not name it but simply call it something else. If we are in denial about one member of an interrelated group or we are simply blind to it, God in His mercy will help us to see. But we still need to take responsibility and name our enemy.

Superficial vs. Significant

Many times the spirits that seem most superficial are really important because they are present to cover up and disguise or hide the more significant ones. Freedom will come when the deepest bondage is uncovered and renounced. Some ministries have listed groupings of spirits and have emphasized discovering the "strongman" or the most powerful spirit that holds the rest together. Our approach is to have the person renounce all the spirits, lies, and bindings that can be identified and then take authority over all spirits that have been renounced. The person will generally know which one had the deepest hold on them.

Naming Your Enemy: The Importance of Precision

Humans have developed numerous words in order to communicate experience more precisely. For example, in Greek, there are four words for love, and in Arctic regions, there are many words describing the different qualities of snow. It is important to use the words that most precisely identify our experience. Knowing the identity of our enemy will help us to have ongoing victory. If we are vague about our enemies, we will have trouble standing in the truth and freedom Christ has given us. Satan will want to steal it. If we know clearly the identity of our enemy, we will be prepared to recognize any attempts to deceive us and regain access or to take back ground we have already taken. Spirits are identified by what they do. They are attached to a sin and/or deception that Jesus has taken to the cross. Once we have surrendered to Jesus and we repent, confess, and renounce the sin and deception we have been in agreement with, the spirit behind it no longer has a place to rest and must leave when commanded in the name of Jesus to go. Jesus is the one who broke Satan's legal right to us when He died for our sins and forgave us for acting on the enemy's deceptions.

Common Associations of Spirits

Becoming familiar with common associations of spirits will help you grow in understanding, but it will not replace the need to listen carefully to the person's story and receive guidance from the Holy Spirit as you help the person name their enemies. Commanding spirits to go based on the list and without personal discernment is a mistake. The enemy may remain hidden regardless of how many spirits are renounced and cast out if we fail to create a safe atmosphere of love and acceptance as we listen to the person's story. **The person must be helped to connect their experience to the identity of the spirit that is influencing or binding them.**

Becoming familiar with groupings as you pray with people is similar to being introduced to a new set of inter-relationships. When you first come into the group, it may not be so clear how the group functions. But over time, you get to know the individuals in the group; you see how they interrelate. You discover the real leader, find out who makes things happen and who get things done, and you learn how the group operates. Growing in understanding of groupings of spirits will increase your God-given gift of discernment. But study is not the primary means to gain understanding. You can study about a person and read books about them and yet you will not really know them until you meet them. In order to grow in discernment, one needs to spend time helping people take hold of their freedom in Christ. Once you encounter a spirit binding a person and see how others are interrelated, you will then be much quicker to recognize the spirits and understand how they work in the future.

I have compiled a list that is intended as an introduction, not a manual. You can use it to reflect upon what the Lord is teaching you as you seek to set the prisoners free. The list is called "Samples of Related Spirits." It can be found in Appendix B, directly following this article, or on our website, www.heartofthefather.com.

I encourage you to look at the list I have compiled and become familiar with it. See how the words connect or are similar to one another. Each person the Lord sends to you is part of your training. You will learn as you serve. You will understand the spirits behind the words as you connect them to experience. I purposely do not look at a list when I minister to someone; I prefer to trust the Holy Spirit and to be engaged in the process of discovery with the person. You may choose another approach.

The intention of this list is to help you listen to another person's story. If you just drive out spirits without the process of helping the person identify their enemies, it is less likely they will be able to hold their freedom. As you put the groupings together, you are helping each person understand the patterns of deception the devil has used to try to keep them from knowing the love of God.

Part 4: Samples of Related Spirits

- ✣ Anger, resentment, bitterness, revenge (or retaliation), hatred, rage, violence, murder, unforgiveness
- ✣ Pride, rebellion, disobedience
- ✣ Pride, self-justification, self-righteousness, perfectionism, striving, stubbornness
- ✣ Pride, arrogance, superiority, willfulness, argumentativeness
- ✣ Insecurity, fear of man, timidity, shyness, self-pity, inadequacy
- ✣ Insecurity, emptiness, nothingness, loneliness, abandonment
- ✣ Rejection, abandonment, orphan spirit, fatherlessness, hurt, insecurity, feeling unwanted
- ✣ Fear of: rejection, abandonment, judgment, condemnation, and accusation
- ✣ Fear, control, anxiety, worry
- ✣ Confusion, self-doubt, frustration, forgetfulness
- ✣ Control, witchcraft
- ✣ Shame, guilt, condemnation, unworthiness, embarrassment, humiliation, worthlessness, accusation
- ✣ Self-accusation, self-condemnation, self-rejection, self-blame self-criticism, self-hatred
- ✣ Loneliness, isolation, withdrawal, self-protection
- ✣ Judgment, criticism, accusation, superiority, comparison, insecurity, fear
- ✣ Lost, homeless, purposelessness, meaninglessness, aimlessness
- ✣ Spirit of infirmity: renounce the spirit behind: cancer, migraines, arthritis
- ✣ Jealousy, envy, selfishness, greed

- Withdrawal, escape, isolation, fantasy
- Suicide, death, abortion, murder
- Depression, self-pity, hopelessness, despair, discouragement, hurt, suicide, emotional pain
- Self-protection, self-dependence, pride, independence
- Mental illness, fear of mental illness
- Doubt, unbelief
- Religious pride, religiosity
- Shame, self-hatred, self-mutilation, sadomasochism
- Laziness, tiredness, weariness
- Perfectionism, pride, self-reliance, independence
- Specific areas of pride (i.e., intellectual pride)
- Grief, sorrow, sadness, crying
- Poverty, failure, hopelessness
- Addictions, alcoholism, nicotine, drugs, gluttony
- Lust, masturbation, fornication, adultery, rape, incest, homosexual encounters, bestiality, worthlessness
- Victim identity, powerlessness, helplessness, self-pity
- Homosexual identity or lifestyle
- Spirit of homosexuality or lesbianism
- Spiritism, spirit guide ("The spirit that came to me when I…")
- False religions
- Occult: Ouija board, palm reading, fortunetelling, astrology, tarot cards (see Appendix 1 in *Unbound*)

Appendix B

Fear is a significant entry point; men and women can be in fear of anything, including every item on the list above. Lead the individual to renounce the lie, the vow, the idol of, the spirit that entered, and so on.

Part 5: Lies to Renounce

The following gives you an idea of the range of lies that may be uncovered in a ministry session. The lies are as unique as the person's story. Reflecting on this list will help you pick up on lies as they are expressed.

Be aware that you can deal with the lies by renouncing the specific lie or renouncing the spirit. For example, the lie "I am a failure" may be dealt with by renouncing a spirit of failure. The lie "I am not a good mother/father" may be dealt with by renouncing self-rejection, self-criticism, self-accusation, and so on. The lie "No one needs me" may be dealt with by renouncing self-pity. It may be helpful to assist a person in naming the spirits behind the statements because you then can name related spirits that may be harassing them. On the other hand, it may be more effective to simply renounce the lie because the words of the lie precisely express their bondage. Your best guide is to listen to the heart of the person in front of you while being led by the Spirit.

Lies:

- *I'm never where I'm supposed to be—I shouldn't be here—I should be dead—I don't belong—I am always in the wrong place*

- *I'll never amount to anything—I'll never be a success—I am a failure*

- *I am of no significance*

- *I have to do it all myself—No one will help me*

- *Nobody cares if I live or die*

- *I have to get it right—I have to be perfect/the best—I can't make a mistake (or something bad will happen)*

- *My mother/father/sister/brother/spouse's illness/death is my fault—I am responsible for their illness/death*

- *I do not have a voice—I am invisible*

- *It is always my fault*

- *Something's wrong with me*

Appendix B

- *I am ugly*
- *I am unworthy*
- *I am a terrible mom*
- *I'm nothing—I don't matter—I'm a mistake—I am worthless—I am not worthy*
- *God won't/can't help me—God doesn't want to help me—God doesn't care about me*
- *God can't be bothered with me*
- *God's mercy/blessing/favor is for everyone but me*
- *God is against me—God wants to punish/ is punishing me—God is getting back at me*
- *God is not in control—I've destroyed God's plan for my life*
- *Someone/everyone is out to get me*
- *My life is cursed—My life is doomed—I've destroyed my life—Bad things always happen to me*
- *I am a victim—I can't do anything right—I'm not able to do anything*
- *God cannot forgive me*
- *I am in control—I can fix those I love*
- *What I want doesn't matter*
- *I am worthless—I am lazy—I am no good—I am garbage*
- *I am not normal*
- *I can't say no—Anyone can do whatever they want to me and I can't say no*
- *I should be punished*
- *Nothing good ever happens or will ever happen to me*
- *I can't do anything about it—I can't fight back—I'm too weak*

- It's hopeless—I can never change
- Showing emotion means I'm weak
- If they knew the real me, no one would like me
- If I say/do the right thing, everyone will be happy
- God made a mistake when He made me a man/woman
- Their anger is my fault
- My father's/mother's/sister's/brother's/spouse's anger/abuse was my fault
- I have to earn God's love
- God has abandoned me—God has rejected me—God is not protecting me—God has forsaken me
- Nothing is ever good enough
- I deserve the abuse
- The enemy/Satan is stronger than God
- God wanted this to happen to me
- No one will ever believe me
- I'm stupid—I'm bad—I'm dirty—I'm shameful—I'm sick—I'm nasty
- I should have stopped them—I deserved it—I should have done something to stop it
- It's just a matter of time before it happens again
- If I let them into my life, they'll hurt me too
- Not even God can help me
- God could never want me because of what happened to me
- I am a burden
- No one needs me—I am unimportant
- God could never love me

- *I'm never going to get any better*
- *I have no reason to live*
- *Heaven is not for me*

Remember, whether a person renounces spirits, lies, or idols, the important thing is verbally breaking any internal agreement with the enemy's plan for their life. They are saying before witnesses, "I'm done with this."

Part 6: Developing an Unbound Ministry

ONE LOCAL TEAM'S STORY: IN THEIR OWN WORDS[1]

UNBOUND prayer is premised on the belief that the gospel can make a difference in a person's life. Neal Lozano preaches the same timeless gospel—but in a way that makes the power of the Word truly accessible to the believer. It is an inspired model of deliverance prayer that guides a person in responding to the gospel and opening their heart more fully to Jesus. A full explanation of this model is given in the book UNBOUND by Neal Lozano, and also presented via the UNBOUND: Freedom in Christ conferences given internationally by Neal and Janet Lozano. (For more information, visit www.heartofthefather.com).

The basic framework of UNBOUND moves the participant through the steps of surrender to Christ. In this model, the *person receiving prayer* is the one doing the work; the prayer minister simply leads the person through the Five Keys:

1. *Repenting for sin and expressing faith in Jesus' power to save*

2. *Extending forgiveness to oneself and others in agreement with the forgiveness given through Jesus Christ*

3. *Renouncing the lies, spirits, and tactics of the enemy*

4. *Taking authority over the works of Satan*

5. *Receiving the Father's blessing*

Those of us who have received a blessing through UNBOUND prayer often have a heart for passing it on to others. My husband and I caught this vision a few years ago at an UNBOUND conference at our church. We decided at that time to develop an ongoing UNBOUND

---

[1] This is not intended to be an official step-by-step manual on how to start a local team, but it contains a great many valuable experiences and insights that may be helpful to you as you develop your team.

ministry there so we could continue praying with people for freedom. Since we attend a Roman Catholic church, our first step was to seek the support of our pastor and align ourselves under his authority. Thankfully, this wasn't too hard, as we were both already active and involved at the parish, and also because our pastor was blessed at the UNBOUND conference himself!

Below, you can read answers to common questions we receive about developing an UNBOUND prayer ministry.

How did we select the team members?

We only invited to the team *people who had already attended some UNBOUND leadership training*. In putting together a team, we looked for people who were willing to commit *time* to further training and to ongoing ministry. At first, our team met monthly and we also hosted monthly ministry sessions at the church—the best way to learn is to practice! We made sure our team was aware of Neal and Janet's conference schedule, and we tried to schedule times when we could travel together to serve at these events. After a year, we decreased the time commitment to meetings every other month, and ministry events seasonally—Advent, Lent, Easter, summer, and on parish retreats.

We looked for prayer leaders who had a *good understanding of the UNBOUND model*. We were aware that people desiring to serve others through UNBOUND ministry might view it through the lens of their own experience. Potential prayer ministers might come to the team already trained and gifted in skills such as pastoral counseling, spiritual direction, inner healing, healing of memories, other approaches to deliverance, empathetic listening, grief counseling, intercessory prayer, or personal support and service. Although elements of all these things are found in the UNBOUND model, UNBOUND is not any of these things. Simply put, UNBOUND prayer helps a person apply the power of the gospel to their story through use of the Five Keys. We needed people who were committed to minister on our team using the UNBOUND model—and *only* the UNBOUND model—as taught by Neal and Janet Lozano. They might use other approaches outside of their UNBOUND service, but we needed to get a clear agreement from people that they would learn and stick to this model when serving at team events.

We invited to the team people *who were mature, who would be discreet*. It is very important to realize that the types of issues people bring to UNBOUND prayer do not fall into the category of your average ministry-after-the-prayer meeting. People are bringing deep pain, deep shame, revealing secrets they often have never revealed to another living soul. We needed members who could listen to just about anything with compassion and not convey shock or disapproval. And, obviously, we needed to have faith our team members would not talk about what they had heard with anyone else after the session.

When putting together our team, we looked for people who were *full of faith*, who could believe God was *already* doing a work in the person coming for prayer and who were ready to bless that work. We needed people who could relax in the Lord. UNBOUND prayer ministers need to realize they are not responsible for results in the prayer session; they are like coaches. "You can do it!" is the rallying cry. As Neal Lozano says, the minister needs to "listen like a parent watching a child at a swim meet"—not like a mother tucking her child into bed. People receiving prayer should leave the session feeling loved and respected no matter what else happens.

Most important, we looked for *humble people*, people who realized that UNBOUND ministry was *not* about the prayer minister. We needed people who did not rely solely on their personal gifts or anointing. We asked people if they were ready to open themselves up to observation, to getting feedback from trainers or teammates after leading a prayer session. Thankfully, just about everyone on our team was not only willing to do that but also really wanted the input.

To review, we invited people to be on the team and did not ask for volunteers. We chose people who were:

✣ Trained in the UNBOUND model and able to devote time to the ministry

✣ Committed to following the UNBOUND model of prayer when ministering on our team

✣ Mature and discreet

✣ Full of faith

✣ Humble

How did we train the team?

We recommend, before starting to train your team, you make sure each member has personally received a complete UNBOUND ministry session and that the team shares their testimonies with one another.

Since the time we built this team, Neal and Janet have published *UNBOUND: Freedom in Christ Companion Guide*. We would highly recommend that any group desiring to form a prayer team go through the guide together, reviewing the conference or book material in more depth.

But at the time we started out, we didn't have the advantage of the study guide, so we just dove in. We had two parts to our team formation:

Practice

As stated above, we organized monthly ministry events at our church. We advertised these in our church bulletin and through word of mouth. However, at the beginning, we set up the sessions a little differently than Neal and Janet would at a conference: we had a prayer leader, an intercessor/observer, *and a trainer,* someone with experience and gifting in UNBOUND prayer ministry.[2]

We made sure we had permission from our team members before assigning them to the role of prayer leader—some really wanted more time to observe before they were ready to lead a session. We also made sure our team had resources to take into the prayer sessions so they would feel more comfortable: practice sheets, note-taking tools, and the list of related spirits.

At the start of each ministry session, we informed the person receiving prayer we were just developing our ministry and the prayer leader was still learning with the input or assistance of the prayer leader as needed. We thanked the person for participating with the training process and reassured them the UNBOUND model didn't depend on the expertise of the prayer leader but simply on our cooperation with the Holy Spirit in using the Five Keys.

---

[2] We recommend that local trainers be observed and receive feedback from a Heart of the Father Ministries trainer, if at all possible. This was not available when this team was developed.

The prayer leader had permission to turn the session over to the trainer at any point where he felt out of his level of confidence, and the prayer leader also understood the trainer could take the reins if it seemed necessary. (We rarely had to do this, but we felt we had to give priority to the freedom of the person receiving prayer over the emotional needs of the prayer minister.)

After the prayer session ended, we allowed ten to fifteen minutes of debrief time for the leader, the observer/intercessor, and the trainer to have a chance to talk about what happened. At this point, the trainer had a chance to give instruction or feedback.

We sent a follow-up email to each person who had received prayer, asking for feedback. Most people responded, and this feedback was invaluable to us in developing the team.

Over the course of several months, every person who initially joined our team had a chance to be observed by all three of our experienced trainers. We mixed up the intercessor/observers and leaders so people could experience a variety of styles and skill levels and resisted settling into permanent teams even though there were definitely people who felt they gelled well with certain team members and wanted to keep praying together. The main effect of this was people realized God worked in the UNBOUND model no matter how talented or experienced the prayer minister was. People gained more confidence that God would come through for them when they stepped out to lead.

The trainers on our team met together every few months to review the progress we were making through training and to "check off" people who we felt were ready to go solo or even to help us with the training process.

Once people were trained and ready to lead, we stopped including a trainer on the teams. We allowed leaders to decide for themselves who would lead each session.

Note: At the beginning of our ministry, everyone was so excited to learn that we often had people requesting to watch the sessions, even if they were not assigned to the ministry teams. We quickly learned people receiving ministry found it hard to really relax and open up with a crowd in the corner even though they wanted to be accommodating and agreed to have extra observers in the room.

We advise sticking to groups of no more than three. Additionally, we instruct our intercessors not to take notes but simply to listen and to pray. When intercessors take notes, they may lose their focus on the person receiving prayer and on the Holy Spirit. The person receiving prayer may feel intimidated if several people are recording the story.

Education

The second prong of our team training was ongoing education. We invited speakers to our team meetings who had expertise in common issues encountered in Unbound prayer ministry. While we understood our role was not to diagnose or to counsel, we felt having an understanding of issues like alcoholism, divorce recovery, or post-abortion trauma would help us to listen more intentionally to the stories and would guide us in asking questions during the interview. For example, the man who spoke to us on alcoholism told us that at heart, "Every alcoholic is deeply afraid." Most of us listening to an alcoholic's story might pick up on anger, rage, pride, defensiveness…but not necessarily fear. Yet this might be at the root of everything else.

We chose only speakers who had some familiarity with Unbound so they could tailor their talks to our needs. We asked our speakers to recommend resources in the area that we could pass on to people who wanted to pursue other avenues of healing after receiving ministry, like counseling or support groups.

Another important educational piece in our monthly meetings was the chance to debrief our own experiences in ministry. While preserving confidentiality by changing names, dates, and details, we needed a chance to talk about things that might have surprised or upset us, and to ask each other, "What would you have done?" Sometimes a prayer team member would ask for prayer if he or she was troubled spiritually or emotionally by how they responded to what was shared during a ministry session.

The leaders of our team stayed in touch with Neal and Janet, getting advice on questions or problems that arose. Occasionally we'd compile a long list of questions and send it off to Neal and Janet for comment, sharing the answers with our group via email or at team meetings.

Did all those who began training in Unbound prayer ministry complete it successfully? What did you do if someone just didn't seem to be cut out for it?

The whole team agreed up front that the trainers had permission to let people know if we thought the ministry was not a good match for their gifts. However, we wanted to let everyone know that if they had a heart for Unbound, then we had a place for them on the team. In the end, some people were led to the role of intercessor rather than prayer leader. Some people ended up choosing an administrative role—a highly needed service! We needed people to schedule the rooms, advertise the events, set up prayer ministry schedules, and plan team meetings. A really important role we discovered was the role of a host or hostess for our ministry sessions, someone to welcome people by greeting them, setting them at ease, showing them where to go for their prayer sessions, offering water or coffee, and creating a peaceful and private environment complete with lots of Kleenex!

Generally, people were well aware of their limitations and most people self-selected into support roles if they found leading prayer ministry challenging. We had a couple of difficult conversations, but we believe we all grew through this honest communication grounded in loving acceptance.

What told you that someone was not a good fit for Unbound ministry? How did you make the decision to guide someone into another role?

As we said above, most people self-selected out of a ministry role if it wasn't right. Generally, there were four common reasons for someone to move into a different role or leave the team:

1. Time constraints—some people were just too busy to come to many events, and we wanted people to be connected to the team and participate in the training. We felt it was too risky to have someone loosely connected to us coming in once in a while to pray with people.

2. Difficulty learning the steps in the model—although there's a definite learning curve in which people need to use guides and suggested conversation starters, some people never got beyond proceeding mechanically through the steps. Using the Five Keys in a rote manner or renouncing related spirits as a "laundry list" can leave the person receiving prayer feeling misunderstood and pushed through the process. The prayer minister needs to be able to make a good relational connection to the person receiving prayer and to respond sensitively to whatever unfolds. A prayer minister must grow in the skill to move fluidly back and forth between the steps as the situation calls for it. For example, sometimes a person cannot forgive or repent until other layers of spiritual influence have been renounced, and the prayer minister will have to back up and start again from the first key with a new area. This is one reason why Neal refers to UNBOUND as a model, not a method.

3. Inability or unwillingness to use only the UNBOUND model—this is the opposite of the previous problem. Some people had strong gifts of prophecy, counsel, etc., and felt that since God had given them these gifts, they needed to use them in the way they were accustomed to. If they were not able to adapt the use of the gift into the context of UNBOUND ministry, we encouraged these people to continue praying and ministering elsewhere. We believed we had a responsibility to be true to the model if we were calling ourselves an UNBOUND ministry so that Neal and Janet's teaching would be legitimately represented.

4. Distress that lingered after the prayer sessions because of the traumatic issues that were described—some prayer ministers, either because of their sensitive natures or their own personal histories, were unable to leave those issues behind.

How do you organize the ministry events?

Our ministry events are usually held on Saturday mornings. We advertise these with flyers in the church bulletin, broadcast email, and/or bulletin announcements. People respond to a contact person to request an appointment; we schedule one and a half hours for each person receiving prayer.

When the schedule coordinator responds to the request, they always ask if the person has read at least the first half of *Unbound* (or heard the teaching through a conference or audio/visual materials). If not, then they ask if it will be possible to do so before the session; if the person doesn't think so, then they encourage the person to wait for the next event. We do this because the sessions are much more fruitful if a person is familiar with the model and comes prepared. After all, it is the person receiving prayer who is really doing the work to take hold of their freedom: we're the facilitators.

Additionally, the coordinator sends a "Preparing to Receive Unbound Ministry" document to the person. This is a tool that helps the person reflect beforehand—it's not something the person turns in or goes over with the prayer minister in the session. Once we confirm an appointment, we take requests for a preferred time slot and get a cell phone number for last-minute changes or problems.

During the same timeframe in which the coordinator is taking requests from people hoping for prayer, they must touch base with the team to confirm who can pray and when. (We use email as the primary communication medium for our team.)

People often think there's some magic about how we make the schedule, some hidden plan or purpose. Honestly, by the time we work around everyone's schedule constraints and personal requests (like, "I don't want so-and-so to pray with me because he's my neighbor"), the schedule just falls into place—at least, that's the hope! We do pray and ask the Holy Spirit to guide us when setting up the prayer sessions, and God always honors that prayer.

Within a day or two of the event, we send a copy of the first draft of the schedule to the team *and* the intercessors just to catch any mistakes and also to remind people of the prayer time. Then we send the final draft to everyone, including our hostess, so she can make signs for the doors and come prepared to greet people. (Note: we only use first names or initials on the schedule since it goes out to so many people or is put up on the walls at the venue.)

Besides these regular ministry events, we schedule private appointments for people who can't come to one or who want to meet sooner than the next event. Sometimes we have people with handicaps who need to meet in their homes. The schedule coordinator takes these requests and then passes them on to the team via broadcast email. When a team member volunteers to lead such a session, responsibility passes to the team member to contact the person, set up a time, and find an intercessor.

HOW DO YOU FOLLOW UP WITH PEOPLE WHO HAVE RECEIVED PRAYER? WHAT INSTRUCTION DO YOU GIVE THEM ABOUT WHAT COMES NEXT?

Occasionally people contact us after a prayer ministry session feeling confused and upset because they experienced agitation due to old memories stirred up. Sometimes they experienced doubt about their freedom or fear that the enemy would retaliate.

Because of this, we have learned to spend some time at the end of each prayer session counseling people about what to expect and how to fight the battle for their minds, and assuring them we are available for questions or further prayer. Here are some of the points we cover at the end of a prayer time:

1. We reassure people that they can repeat the process on their own. If something comes up later, if they feel tested or harassed, they can repent, forgive, renounce the evil one with authority, and ask for the Father's blessing. The five keys are in their hands.

2. We also advise them that the greatest protection against the enemy is gratitude and praise for what God has done and trust for what is to come. We encourage them to go home and journal about what has happened for them through UNBOUND prayer, perhaps using the prayer leader's note sheet. We ask them to take some time (immediately after the session, if possible) to go and pray with thanksgiving to the Father. And we ask them to share about their new freedom with at least one other person!

3. We remind people receiving UNBOUND prayer that they have moved from "a place of bondage to a place of weakness." Weakness is a place of dependency on the Lord, a place where intimacy with

Him can grow. It's nothing to be afraid of! "Fear is useless; what is needed is faith!"

4. We offer people a chance to purchase Ann Stevens' talk on "Staying Free," available from Heart of the Father Ministries. We encourage them to listen to it within the week.

5. Finally, we later developed a follow-up sheet for people to take home after the ministry time. In it we write:

Some people experience amazing joy and transformation after UNBOUND prayer; it culminates a long process of healing. For others the initial UNBOUND session is a first step leading to future opportunities for greater liberation. Becoming aware of these areas may feel unsettling, but it does not mean you have lost what God gave you. Often it means you are ready for more. Give thanks; use the Keys for yourself or with a friend. Feel free to call the person who prayed with you to share your ongoing liberation process. And remember God's Word: "Trust in the LORD with all your heart and lean not on your own understanding; in all your ways acknowledge Him, and He will make your paths straight" (Proverbs 3:5-6).

Postscript

The Way Forward: Ongoing Unbound Ministry Training

It is my hope that once you have been trained in UNBOUND ministry, you will continually train others. You have given away the freedom you have received in Christ; now give the ministry away to more and more people. Heart of the Father Ministries has many resources to help you provide a solid foundation for the ministry of others. What is the best way to utilize these resources? We suggest the following as an ideal path of training.

STUDY: Most people begin by reading *UNBOUND: A Practical Guide to Deliverance*, and many follow that by receiving personal ministry. We encourage you to make use of other resources as well, such as the UNBOUND: Freedom in Christ conference CDs or DVDs and the companion guide that includes detailed talk notes, daily meditations, and testimonies. We have also placed our conference ministry team training onto DVD and CD format. For those who want to know more about how evil spirits work and gain deeper insight into the development of deliverance ministry in church history and in the Catholic Church, see Neal's book *Resisting the Devil: A Catholic Perspective on Deliverance*. He wrote this book specifically for Catholics, but it offers biblical and historical insights that would benefit all.

ATTEND: The Freedom in Christ conference gives everyone an opportunity to engage in the message of UNBOUND in an atmosphere of worship and faith. By receiving ministry, each person will learn how to help others receive freedom since clear teaching on the basics of how to receive deliverance and how to help others is given at each conference. For information on hosting a conference, go to www.heartofthefather.com.

SERVE: The best way to train people in UNBOUND ministry is to do it in connection with a conference. Not only will leaders-in-training be able to receive ministry themselves, but they also can participate in ministry to others under the guidance of experienced prayer ministers. Local groups planning to host a conference usually send a few leaders to an UNBOUND: Freedom in Christ conference. Upon their return home, they prepare a group of leaders to serve as a ministry team for their UNBOUND conference by having the ministry team members read *UNBOUND* and attend a series of group meetings where they receive teaching by watching and discussing conference and training DVDs. As they learn, they begin to minister to one another in small groups. During the conference itself, the Heart of the Father Ministries team will meet with the leaders to answer any immediate or significant questions. This is followed by ninety-minute ministry sessions during the day on Friday when the leaders, in groups of three or four, observe a ministry session led by a Heart of the Father team member before discussing the process. On Friday night and Saturday of each conference, new ministry leaders will learn by listening and doing. They will pray for conference participants following each talk on the keys and they will participate in private UNBOUND sessions on Saturday afternoon.

PRACTICE: Because of time constraints at conferences, it is common for there to be many people who request personal ministry but do not receive it. Follow-up ministry sessions for these individuals should be scheduled. The greatest learning comes as we continue to minster to others and then receive feedback from team members. We recommend avoiding integration of the UNBOUND model with other healing and deliverance ministry methods for three to six months following the conference. This time allows the trained ministry team members to discover the power of each of the keys and grow in understanding and in confidence.

DEVELOP LOCAL TEAMS: When the conference ends, it is the opportune time for a local, permanent ministry team to form. Local team leaders can consult with the pastor or those in pastoral authority to receive their blessing and guidance on forming a team. At this point, the decision is made whether the new UNBOUND ministry team will function within the church itself or as an outreach of the local body. This new ministry will require leaders who can serve as trainers. These leaders observe ministry; give feedback; and help people to find their place on the ministry team as administrator, prayer leader, intercessor, leader in training, or helper. People who volunteer to join the team should know who the leaders are and what their responsibility is for developing the team. If someone is more suited for another type of healing ministry, he should be blessed and encouraged to move in that direction. This begins the process of establishing an UNBOUND ministry team that will be an ongoing resource for the local church and beyond.

FOLLOW UP WITH TRAINING AND RESOURCES: The Heart of the Father Ministries team is available to visit your new ministry if you so wish. We can answer questions, observe the team in ministry work, and provide feedback on your progress. Prior to this visit, the local team should read and discuss the *UNBOUND MINISTRY Guidebook*.

New opportunities for training will be made available through **www.heartofthefather.com** and notice will be given through our free email updates, accessible via the "Newsletter Sign-Up" on our website.

Updates to this guidebook, including information about using the UNBOUND name, as well as the rest of the ministry documents and tools from Appendix B (listed on pages 199–200) can be found online at **www.heartofthefather.com.**

BIOGRAPHICAL SKETCHES

NEAL LOZANO has more than thirty-five years of pastoral experience helping people find freedom in Christ. He is the author of the best-selling book, UNBOUND: *A Practical Guide to Deliverance*. An international speaker, Neal has spoken at seminars and conferences throughout the world. Married since 1973, Neal and his wife Janet live in Ardmore, Pennsylvania. They have four sons and nine grandchildren.

Neal holds a master's degree in religious education from Villanova University, where he also led an evangelistic outreach to students for eighteen years.

Currently, Neal is serving as senior coordinator for the House of God's Light, an ecumenical Christian community which he has served since 1975. Over the years, Neal has become a respected authority in deliverance ministry, developing a unique and balanced approach which includes detailed biblical grounding, real-life examples, and immense practicality.

Neal, a Roman Catholic, has had extensive experience ministering across the body of Christ. Neal and his wife Janet are committed to being instruments of the Father's Love.

MATTHEW LOZANO is a gifted speaker and teacher who trains leaders to use the UNBOUND model for ministry. Matt recently joined the staff of Heart of the Father Ministries part-time as a prayer team trainer and resource developer. Over the past fifteen years, he has served various ministries including Intervarsity Christian Fellowship, Lifeteen, and Renewal Ministries. A Social Studies teacher with a Master's degree in Education, Matt is currently working on his Master's degree in Biblical Theology. He and his wife Jenn, who also works for Heart of the Father Ministries, have four children and live in the Philadelphia area.

UNBOUND MINISTRY: If you or your ministry team are already using the UNBOUND Model, we would love to hear about your experiences and stay in touch with you. Please email us with a brief description of your ministry and include your contact information: info@heartofthefather.com. Be sure to sign up for our newsletter, found on our website.

ADDITIONAL RESOURCES: To purchase additional resources, go to www.heartofthefather.com and click on the link: "Store"

ITEMS CURRENTLY AVAILABLE:

- *Ministry Team Training* (DVDs and CDs available)
- *UNBOUND: Freedom in Christ Conference* (DVD series, updated March 2011)
- *UNBOUND: Freedom in Christ Companion Guide* (workbook for the conference series)
- Digital Downloads—conference audios available in MP3 format
- *UNBOUND: A Practical Guide to Deliverance* (book)
- *Resisting the Devil: A Catholic Perspective on Deliverance* (book)
- *The Older Brother Returns: Finding a Renewed Sense of God's Love and Mercy* (book)

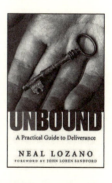